NEW TECHNIQUES AND APPROACHES

FOR

WOOD CARVING

D. V. SEMENICK

WITH 126 ILLUSTRATIONS

copyright © 1986 Dan V. Semenick

Heartwood Books
P.O. Box 1340, Station A,
Delta, British Columbia,
Canada.
V4M 3Y8

This book was typeset by Design Typesetting Ltd., Victoria, B.C., designed by Dan V. Semenick, and printed and bound in Canada by Hemlock Printers Ltd. for Heartwood Books.

The cover photograph was taken by Richard Hackett.

The text photographs were taken by Peter Nielsen, Richard Hackett and by the author.

First printing July 1986
Canadian Cataloguing in Publication Data
Semenick, D.V. (Danny Victor), 1933-
   New techniques and approaches for wood
carving

ISBN 0-9692582-0-8
1. Wood-carving — Technique. I. Title.
NK9704.S44 1986   736'.4'028   C86-091409-7

I wish to dedicate this book to the memory of my father, "Big Bill" Semenick who spent most of his life as a blacksmith.

He taught me how to work with my hands, but most important, he taught me not only to respect the tools of the craftsman, but to respect the craftsman himself.

CONTENTS

ACKNOWLEDGMENTS

I extend my special thanks to my wife Joan and to my daughters Kim and Chris for making this book a reality. Their efforts in all aspects of this endeavour from the writing, proofreading, typing, photography etc. have made this book possible.

FORWARD

This book is the fulfillment of a promise to the many carvers and would-be carvers who have watched me carving the "old work boot".

It was during these wood carving demonstrations that I became aware of just how enthusiastic people are to learn this form of art. There were many questions asked about every aspect of wood carving with topics ranging from proper wood selection to making a carver's knife.

After answering their questions, I would be asked to recommend a book on the subject of wood carving. They wanted a book that would summarize the answers that I had given them and also guide them through a detailed carving with step by step instructions. I did not realize how difficult it was to make this recommendation.

This frustration that I felt when I could not refer them to a specific book on wood carving, coupled with their words of encouragement for me to write a book, finally resulted in this book.

It is my sincere wish that this book will live up to the expectations of the many people who convinced me that I should write this book.

I have tried to make the initial exposure to wood carving as complete as possible for anyone who is just beginning to carve wood.

For those of you who are already sharing the enjoyment of wood carving, I hope that the contents of this book will serve as my contribution to your never ending search for new wood carving techniques and new approaches to wood carving.

Dan Semenick.

WOOD SELECTION

These are some of the questions that people have asked me at carving shows and in my carving shop.

"How do you get such detail in your carving?"

"How do you get this so thin on your carving without it breaking?"

"Is the wood that you are using balsa wood? You make it look so soft and easy to carve."

While part of the answer to these questions is, of course, that my tools are sharp, I always give the majority of the credit to the wood that I use. That wood is basswood which is also known as linden. If I were unable to purchase basswood for my carving projects, I am afraid that I might consider another profession entirely.

It would be difficult to find another wood that is as suitable for wood carving as basswood. When each of the requirements for a good wood for carving is reviewed, it is basswood that ends up at the top of the list. I refer to it as the wood carver's wood.

Because basswood is a deciduous tree, it falls into the category of hardwoods. When I am asked whether it is a hardwood or a softwood, I usually pause and say to myself, "Oh no, not again." The correct answer to their question, would seem to be that "basswood is in the hardwood family but it is not hard to carve." This has been my answer on a few occasions when I had simply forgotten what the response of some people would be to such an answer. "See George — I told you that he was carving a softwood. That's why he's cutting that wood so easily" someone whispers in the crowd. I know that there are carvers who, at this point in my book, are chuckling because they have been in this situation also. How does one say that a wood is not hard to carve and then try to convince the crowd that it is not easy to carve? There have been times when I have simply hated the basswood tree for placing me in such a predicament. I have tried to make a point here about how to describe whether basswood is easy to carve or not. First of all, it is in the hardwood family. However, if basswood is being cut with sharp knives and chisels, then I would have to say that it is not difficult to carve. The difficulty in carving basswood only lies in the wood carver's inability to use his tools effectively.

Basswood is virtually free of wood grain which would normally dictate how much detail the wood carver is able to achieve on the finished carving. If the carver's tools are very sharp, there is almost no limit to the detail that the wood carver will be able to incorporate into the carving. The saying that "if it can't be carved in basswood, it just can't be carved in wood", is very close to the truth. For the new wood carver, the ability of basswood to hold detail is very important.

Another reason for recommending basswood to the wood carver is that the wood is receptive to most wood finishes. The absence of pronounced growth rings produces a carving that is uniform in color and free of dark growth lines at regular intervals. Most cedar wood is a good example of a wood with pronounced growth rings. This same wood does not hold detail very well and should not be considered for intricate wood carvings.

To summarize, basswood is relatively easy to cut, will hold the required detail on a carving, and looks beautiful when the final finish is applied.

I have never started a student on his or her first project with any other wood but basswood. A beginner carver has enough to learn without trying to carve a wood that splits or is too hard and will not hold a certain degree of detail.

I strongly recommend that, if you intend to start wood

carving, you select basswood as your first choice for the reasons that have been listed. If it means that you must order some from mail order suppliers because it does not grow in your area, then do so. You will never regret the extra effort and possibly the slight additional cost required to get the basswood.

There are many carving books on the market that list other woods which are suitable for carving along with the properties of each. When you find a need for a different wood, for whatever reason in the future, you can acquaint yourself with it at that time. The wood that you choose will be governed usually by what you will be attempting to carve. The decoy carver, for example, will put basswood, tupelo and pine at the top of his or her list. Carvers of other subjects may rank walnut high on their list and so on.

My advice is that if you are beginning to carve and wish to carve the project in this book, you should find a source for a piece of basswood of sufficient size to cut your carving blank. You will not be fair to yourself if you choose any other wood at this time.

SHARPENING CHISELS

Normally the chapter dealing with Selecting Chisels would preceed the chapter on Sharpening Chisels. In this case however, their order has been changed because the method used to sharpen a chisel has a direct bearing on the selection of the chisel.

More than ten years ago, while attending a wood carving class, I was introduced to a method of sharpening chisels that was a total departure from the traditional method of sharpening as I knew it. The Canadian instructor of this particular wood carving class had attended carving classes in Germany, where he was introduced to the rubber wheel method of honing.

At first glance, I was skeptical of this new approach. I found it hard to believe that years of traditional tool sharpening with oil stones, etc. could be replaced by a simple rubber wheel. After trying the rubber wheel for myself, all of my doubts disappeared. It was amazing! I honed a chisel and had it ready for carving in less than thirty seconds. No oil stones, no leather strops, no messy oil and no clean up. I simply flipped a switch on the motor, which was connected to a grinder head by a V belt, touched the chisel edge to the rubber wheel, and there it was. I had an edge that was a pleasure to use on my carvings, equal to any that I had previously attained using traditional sharpening methods. I have not used anything but the rubber wheel since that day.

For me, carving has always been a great source of enjoyment. Before I discovered the rubber wheel method of honing however, the sharpening of chisels had been a tedious and frustrating procedure. I am sure that most wood carvers feel the same way.

As I have already mentioned, at the time that I was introduced to the rubber wheel, it was mounted on a grinding head which was connected to an electric motor by a V belt. I found that this system was extremely awkward to move around the shop or to take outdoors on nice days when I wanted to carve in the sunshine.

Convinced that there must be a better way to drive this rubber wheel, I designed a unit which is basically a motor mounted on a base, thus eliminating the V belt and the grinder head. This new unit is easy to move around the shop and to take to carving shows because it is so compact (Illus. 2-1).

The first and most basic requirement of this unit was to have the wheels rotating up and away from the operator and not down and toward the operator, as is normal on grinding units (Illus. 2-2). When using rubber honing wheels, leather wheel strops or buffing wheels, the rotation *must* be up and away from the operator. This is necessary because if the wheel rotates down and toward the operator, which is the case with conventional grinding units, the sharp chisel or knife edge would cut into the rubber wheel, destroying the wheel and possibly causing injury to the operator.

Another important feature of this unit is that it has protective wheel covers. I am always concerned when I read articles and instructions on sharpening, in various carving books and magazines, in which wheels are simply mounted on open motor shafts (Illus. 2-3). With virtually no protection for the operator, it is only a matter of time before an injury will take place. A material flaw in the wheel, or the overtightening of a wheel can cause a wheel to break with disastrous results. The wheel covers on this unit are heavy alloy die cast aluminum and are the exhaust type.

Another feature of this unit is that it has been designed to take a 6″ × 1″ wheel as well as the usual 6″ × ¾″ wheel. Most 6″

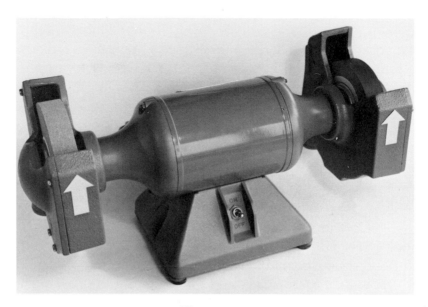

Illus. 2-1

My sharpening unit with a fine grinding wheel and a rubber honing
wheel mounted on the unit.

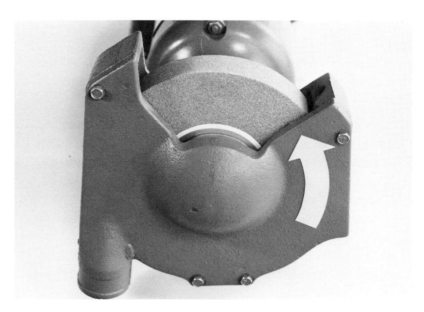

Illus. 2-2

An end view of the wheel cover. Note the rotational direction of the
wheel and the position of the wheel cover opening. The exhaust
opening is at the back of the wheel cover.

Illus. 2-3

Not only is this arrangement for grinding illegal, but it is also dangerous for both the operator and any spectators.

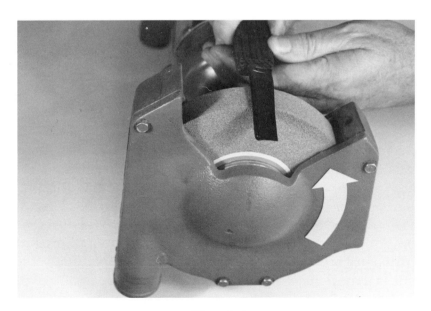

Illus. 2-4

A barber's straight razor being ground to make a carver's knife. The wood handle is being held over the motor which indicates that both sides of the blade can be ground on this unit.

grinding units are restricted to the 6″ × ¾″ wheel only. A wider wheel, whether used for grinding, honing or buffing, provides more surface area and, therefore, more control than a narrow wheel.

When I started grinding and honing on my prototype, I positioned the opening of the wheel cover at the *top* of the wheel, and not at the front as is normally the case on grinders (Illus. 2-2). Anyone sharpening chisels or knives would only have to use this position once to appreciate the tremendous advantage of this new approach. This unit has fixed wheel covers, with the opening positioned at the top of the wheel and slightly toward the operator.

An additional feature of this unit, which will be especially valuable to knife makers and knife sharpeners, is that the wheels are extended from the motor housing and base in lateral distance. This allows grinding and honing on each face of the knife blade (Illus. 2-4). This is a feature that has been overlooked by the manufacturers of most grinding units in the past because the needs of the wood carver were unknown to them.

There is little dispute regarding the merits of the revolutionary rubber wheel method of honing. This unit completes the new sharpening concept by combining the rubber wheel method of honing and the entirely new approach to the grinding procedure for chisels and knives.

Sharpening a chisel on this new unit is very simple and involves only two operations, namely grinding and honing.

Grinding

When using an abrasive grinding wheel on this unit, the grinding approach is entirely different from existing grinding methods. The direction of the wheel rotation is now up and away from the operator and, for those who have been grinding using the standard grinder direction, this approach is new in itself. To add to this new grinding approach, the opening of the wheel cover is at the top of the wheel. The chisel is now held in a more horizontal postion when it is being ground on the wheel. The operator will find that this is a more natural and comfortable position to be in when grinding the chisel edge. This also allows maximum visibility for viewing the edge while grinding (Illus. 2-5).

Because of the position of the wheel cover openings, the unit can be used comfortably on standard height tables such as those provided at carving shows. With standard grinders, it is very awkward to grind the chisel edge when the grinder is sitting on a low table.

Grinding is only necessary to restore the bevel to the edge of a chisel that has lost its required shape through use. You will find that, with several honings on your honing wheel, the bevel on the chisel tends to roll forward. At this point the chisel edge must be ground to a sharp bevel before being honed again.

The angle of the bevel on a chisel is partly determined by the operation that you will be performing with that chisel. The spoon gouge, for example, will not have a sharp angle or be ground back as much as a straight chisel would normally be (Illus. 2-6). This is because the spoon gouge is used with a rolling action on concave cuts, while the straight chisel is used on flat or convex surfaces.

There have been many articles that contain exact sharpening angles for chisels, but I suggest that each wood carver establish his or her own chisel angles based on:

1) The carving operation. For example, is the cut concave, convex or flat?
2) The chisel being used.
3) The type of wood being carved. For example, the chisel edge can be ground to a sharper angle when used on a softer wood.

For grinding chisels, I recommend a 6" × 1" fine grinding wheel with an abrasive number of at least 100. When grinding a chisel on a fine wheel, use very little pressure in order to keep the metal from overheating. The chisel must be kept cool at all times during the grinding process, by dipping it into cold water after every few seconds on the wheel. To keep the water cold, place a few ice cubes in the water container.

Grind along the entire bevel, and right up to the cutting edge of the chisel. If the grinding has been done properly, a burr will form along the entire edge of the chisel. At this point the chisel is ready to be honed.

It is important that fine grinding wheels be dressed often

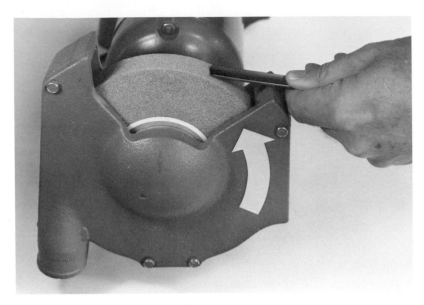

Illus. 2-5

Grinding the bevel on a chisel. Maximum visibility for viewing the edge, while grinding, is achieved with this unit.

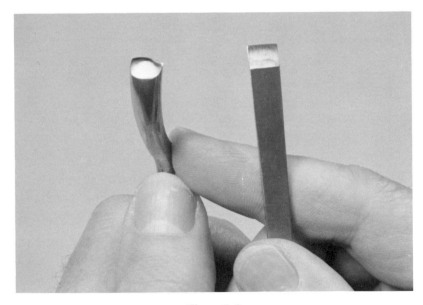

Illus. 2-6

The angle of the bevel on a chisel will vary as shown in this comparison between the spoon gouge and the straight chisel.

Illus. 2-7

A carborundum stick is used for dressing a grinding wheel. This particular stick is 6″ long × ¾″ in diameter and can be adjusted for the amount of projection required.

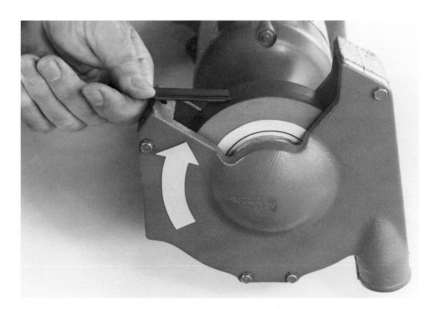

Illus. 2-8

Honing the edge of the chisel on the rubberized abrasive wheel. The chisel is almost in a horizontal position here but the position of the chisel will vary slightly depending on the height of the unit from the floor.

to expose a fresh grinding surface on the wheel. This reduces the risk of overheating the chisel while grinding. The dressing of the wheel is also necessary to "true" the surface of the wheel. Always keep the grinding face flat and as square as possible with the outside faces of the wheel. When dressing the grinding wheel, I prefer to use the carborundum stick rather than the star wheel or diamond wheel dressers (Illus. 2-7).

Honing:

The honing operation is done on a special rubber wheel that has been specifically designed to provide a keen edge on the wood carver's cutting tools. There are some rubberized abrasive wheels on the market that are much too hard and too abrasive, and I must emphasize to you that these are not the wheels that I am referring to in this book. I have tried to hone my cutting edges on these wheels, but I found that they failed to remove the burr that was left from the grinding operation, and they did not leave a highly polished cutting edge.

To hone your chisel on the rubber wheel, simply touch the leading edge of the chisel to the rotating wheel and apply light and even pressure (Illus. 2-8). It is not necessary to polish the entire ground bevel of the chisel. Hone the edge only, as this is where the cutting of the wood is performed. Try a sample cut and if required, retouch the edge of the chisel on the honing wheel until it is super sharp. It should take approximately twenty seconds to hone a chisel.

I prefer a 3450 r.p.m. unit because less tool pressure is required on the wheel when using the higher speed. I feel that this speed provides a keener edge when honing.

Since grinding and honing on this unit is so fast and easy, the wood carver will find that he or she can maintain a superior cutting edge at all times.

SELECTING CHISELS

There are basically two approaches to sharpening a chisel, which in turn will influence what brand of chisel the wood carver will select. The traditional method of sharpening a chisel with stones of various types and grades is slow and messy, however it does result in a more durable cutting edge. A chisel that has been sharpened using the traditional method will retain its edge for a longer period of time than one that has been sharpened using the motorized sharpening method. For this traditional method, chisels made of the harder steel should be selected. It will take more time to sharpen a harder chisel but the extra effort will usually result in a more durable cutting edge. How much more durable the edge will be, is open to discussion.

The harder steel in these chisels is not as suitable as the slightly softer steel in other chisels for motorized sharpening methods. The harder chisel heats up more quickly on the grinding wheel and tends to skip or vibrate on the rubber honing wheel. Most carvers today are willing to sacrifice a certain degree of durability on their chisel edge for a faster sharpening system. They contend that although they must sharpen their chisels more often, they can sharpen their chisels much faster. In the final analysis, they are spending more time on the carving itself.

The carver must therefore decide when selecting chisels, whether a prize winning and slightly more durable edge done by the slow traditional method, is preferred over the very fast motorized method.

If you are just beginning to carve, and you are unfamiliar with various brands of chisels, never buy a complete set of chisels. I suggest that you buy a chisel only when the need to have that chisel arises. There are far too many carvers who, after buying full sets of chisels, end up with certain chisels that never get used. It is far better to have the need arise for a specific chisel and then purchase a chisel for that very purpose. In most cases, the price of the individual chisel is the same price as the identical chisel found in a set, thus offering little or no savings to the buyer.

Purchase a single chisel of a certain brand which is approximately 8 m.m. to 10 m.m. in width, as wider chisels are usually more expensive. Now sharpen this chisel and test it on the wood that you will be using for most of your work. Test other brands in the same way and then select the brand of chisel that you have judged to be the best for you.

The next suggestion is, in my opinion, just as important. Select a chisel that does not have factory grinding marks on the inside face or the cutting face of the chisel (Illus. 3-1). When a bevel is ground on a chisel, this bevel meets the inside face of the chisel. It is at this point where the two surfaces meet that the cutting edge is formed. When the bevelled edge is honed on the rubber honing wheel, a sharp cutting edge should be the result. However, if a chisel has factory grinding marks on the inside face, these grooves will become part of the cutting edge. If you do buy a chisel with the grinding marks on the inside face, it will be necessary to remove these marks before you begin to bevel your chisels. This is time consuming and unnecessary because certain manufacturers of chisels do have polished inside faces, free of grinding marks that would affect your final cutting edge. A chisel manufacturer should provide a well polished inside surface so that you will not have to remove these grinding marks yourself. After all, you are paying for the chisel so this factory operation should be completed.

The wood carver must next determine how much heavy mallet work he or she will be using on the subjects that are being carved. To avoid splitting the chisel handle when using the mallet, the carver must look at the method in which the chisel is mounted into the handle. For heavy work, the shoulder on the tang of the chisel should be substantial. There should be a sturdy metal

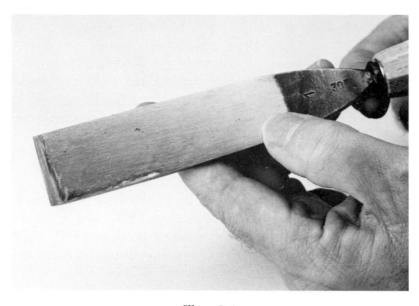

Illus. 3-1

Inspect the inside face of the chisel. Try to purchase chisels that are highly polished and free of deep grinding marks on this face.

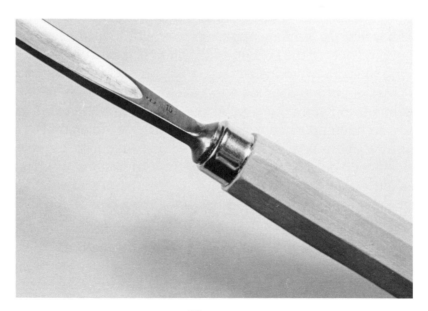

Illus. 3-2

This chisel has a large tang and a strong metal ferrule, which is necessary for chisels which are used along with a mallet for carving.

ferrule on the handle where the tang is set into the chisel (Illus. 3-2). The handle should be made of sound wood to prevent splitting.

If the above mentioned points are equal on the chisels that you have looked at, select the chisel that feels most comfortable in your hand.

MAKING A CARVER'S KNIFE

As a boy, I felt that the jackknife was just about the finest tool ever invented by man. Just imagine, I could take this knife and reduce any piece of wood to a mound of chips in no time at all. There were occasional works of art such as a gun like Roy Rogers had or a sailboat to sail those oceans formed by rain puddles.

The jackknife is still popular today and has many useful purposes. There are carvers who can create some beautiful carvings with this basic knife.

It is my belief that the intricacy of the carvings being created today has placed new demands on the carver's knife. Unfortunately, the jackknife cannot meet these demands. The shape of the blade on the jackknife does not allow it to roll with a concave cut which is, in my opinion, the most basic of knife cuts. This cut is used in many instances on the boot carving in this book, and this same cut would be difficult to execute with the jackknife.

The handle of the jackknife is not suited for hours of continuous carving because the blades, which are partly folded into the handle, tend to dig into the fingers of the hand that is holding the knife.

In addition, the jackknife does not offer enough blade shapes and sizes to complete most intricate carvings (Illus. 4-1).

Eventually the serious wood carver must make his or her own knives or purchase them from a knife maker who makes knives specifically for the wood carver.

Although the steps for making a knife may seem simple, the procedure demands a great deal of patience. I have given some carvers my instructions for knife grinding, only to have them not follow these instructions. The results have been disastrous. I firmly believe that anyone who can make a good carving knife can also be successful at wood carving, because he or she has displayed the most important characteristic needed to do both successfully and that characteristic is patience.

I have used the barber's straight razor for my knife blades since I began making my own knives some ten years ago. I prefer a Solingen steel blade which is only manufactured in Germany but most straight razors, regardless of origin, will produce a good carver's knife.

Some knife makers use power hacksaw blades, which are used in machine shops, for their knife blades. Once these hacksaw blades are dull or have been broken, most shops will give them to a knife maker free of charge. There are other knife makers who use old files for their blades.

I will outline the procedure for making a carver's knife using the straight razor and I hope that the basic steps can be applied to your further adventures in knife making.

ITEMS REQUIRED TO MAKE A CARVER'S KNIFE

1. A BARBER'S STRAIGHT RAZOR.
   Straight razors are still available at the older barber shops. If they are slightly chipped on the edge of the blade, or the handle is broken, they become even easier to get or at least to bargain for (Illus. 4-2). The barber cannot use these defective razors but the wood carver certainly can. Surface rust on the blade will be ground off so don't let the appearance of the blade influence your decision to purchase the razor (Illus. 4-3).

2. TWO PIECES OF HARDWOOD.
   Two pieces of hardwood are required for each knife handle. The size of each piece is 6″ long, 1″ wide and 5/16″ thick. The two surfaces which will be glued together, must be perfectly flat. Any good hardwood will do for the

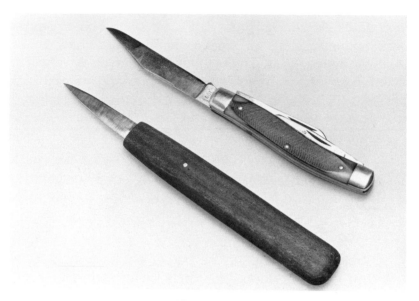

Illus. 4-1

The carver's knife meets all of the demands of the wood carver.
The jackknife is not suited for most of the intricate work
found on today's carvings.

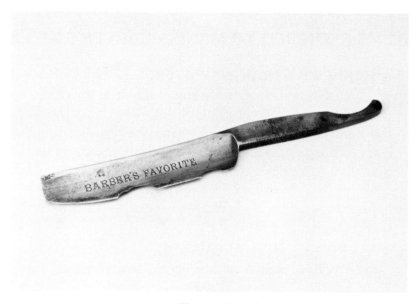

Illus. 4-2

A straight razor with a chipped blade can still be used to make a
carver's knife because this chipped area will be ground off when
shaping the knife blade.

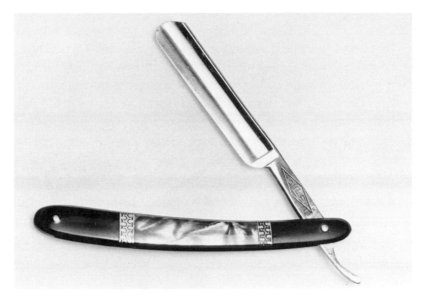

Illus. 4-3

A straight razor with a perfect handle. Unfortunately, the handle must be removed because it is only the blade that is required for the carver's knife.

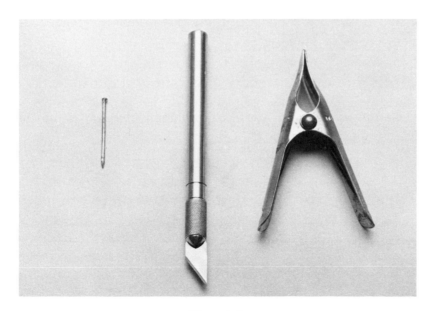

Illus. 4-4

The finishing nail, the X-Acto knife and the spring clamp.

handle but look in the scrap bins of specialty wood shops for exotic pieces. These shops will usually give you a few pieces of wood considering how small the pieces are that you require. I use ebony wood obtained from a guitar builder for my knife handles. Use the nicest pieces of wood that you can find because the wood will give you a sense of pride in your knife before you even start.

3. A WOOD WORKER'S FINISHING NAIL.

The nail must be of such a diameter that it will pass through the handle pivot hole in the tang of the razor (Illus. 4-4). I have used a brass nail on occasion to compliment a special knife. Do not select a nail that would be tight in the hole because it could split the steel tang. Remember that the razor is made of hard and brittle steel. Dropping a straight razor on a hard floor can also break the blade.

4. A BOTTLE OF WHITE GLUE.

Use white glue to glue the pieces of wood that make up the knife handle. I have experimented with all types of glue including epoxy but I still trust the white glue that can be bought in most stores. It has never failed me yet. I have knives that I have used for ten years, with the blades well worn but the handles of the knives have not parted.

5. A SET OF CLAMPS.

I use six small bar type clamps to apply uniform pressure over the entire glue joint on the handle. C type clamps will work just as well. Large clamps become awkward to work with for this glueing operation, so try to use approximately 3″ clamps.

6. A 4 m.m. STRAIGHT CHISEL.

The 4 m.m. wide straight chisel is used to hollow the recess for the straight razor tang in the two pieces of wood that form the knife handle (Illus. 4-5). Depending on the size of the tang, there may be a need for a 2 m.m. wide chisel also. Palm handled chisels work well for this step because they can be controlled more easily than long chisels.

7. AN X-ACTO KNIFE.

It seems ironic to be recommending a craft store

item such as the x-acto knife, for use in the making of a top quality carver's knife (Illus. 4-4). The x-acto knife does, however, work very well for the vertical cut to be made on the outline of the tang which is traced on the two pieces of wood. The x-acto blades are replaceable just in case a tip is broken when you are outlining the tang on the hardwood. I recommend a No. 24 x-acto blade for these vertical cuts.

8. A PAIR OF SIDE CUTTING PLIERS.

The pliers are used to snip off the excess length of the finishing nail that serves as the rivet in the handle. A hacksaw can be used instead of the pliers to trim the nail to length.

9. A GRINDING UNIT.

A motorized grinding unit is, along with the bandsaw, the most used piece of machinery in my shop. It can be used for grinding, honing, buffing and polishing. It is an absolute must to perform the grinding required to make a carver's knife. If you do not have a grinding unit, try to get access to one. I cannot imagine trying to grind a carver's knife with a hand operated unit although I am sure that it can and has been done. I recommend a 6″ grinding unit with a speed of 3450 r.p.m.

10. A 6″ × 2″ OILSTONE.

The purpose of the oil stone is to flatten the two faces of the knife blade and to remove the grinding marks.

11. A 6″ × 2″ RUBBERIZED ABRASIVE BLOCK.

This is the sharpening block that I use for all of my knife honing (Illus. 4-6). With this block, I find that I can match the cutting edges attained using other honing devices such as stones, leather strops etc.

12. A SMOOTH CUT RASP.

The rasp is used to shape the wood handle. It cuts faster than the wood file and reduces the time spent on this procedure. I first started to use this special rasp for shaping guitar necks. It removes the wood quickly but leaves a remarkably smooth finish considering the cut. I would highly recommend this No. 50 smooth cut patternmaker's rasp to all wood carvers who use a rasp to shape their carving

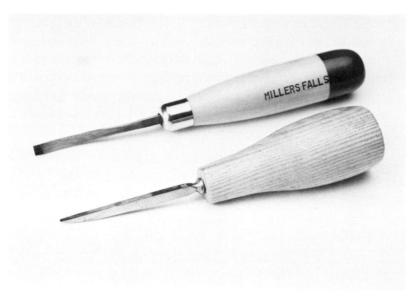

Illus. 4-5

The chisels that I use to make the recesses in the knife handle.

Illus. 4-6

The 6″ × 2″ × ¼″ rubberized abrasive block that is used for honing the blade.

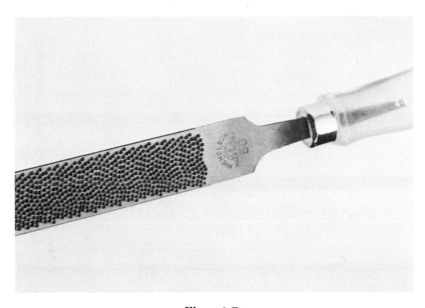

Illus. 4-7

Use a No. 50 smooth cut patternmaker's rasp to shape the handle
of the knife.

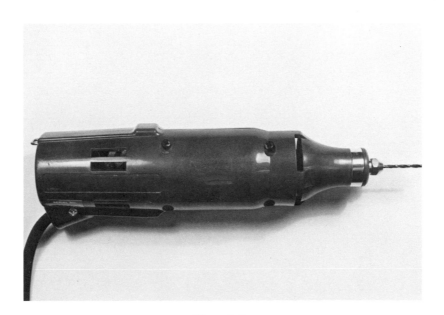

Illus. 4-8

The hobby drill is available at most craft stores and is the ideal size
for drilling small holes.

subjects (Illus. 4-7).

13. A SPRING CLAMP.

      Select a clamp that has a strong spring for maximum holding power (Illus. 4-4). A strong clamp will prevent the tang from slipping as you trace the outline of the tang onto the piece of wood.

14. A SMOOTH FILE AND SANDPAPER.

      These can be used to remove the rasp marks if you wish to have a smoother finish on your knife handle. I prefer the slight roughness left by the smooth cut rasp because the rough surface provides a better grip on the handle.

15. A DRILL AND DRILL BIT.

      Any electric hand drill can be used to drill the holes required for the finishing nail which serves as the rivet in the knife handle. I use a hobby drill because it is easy to handle (Illus. 4-8). These hobby drills are available at most craft stores, hardware stores and major department stores. The drill bit should be the diameter of the finishing nail.

STEPS FOR MAKING A CARVER'S KNIFE

Illus. 4-9

All the items necessary to make the carver's knife.

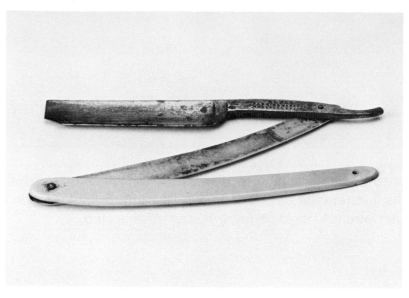

Illus. 4-10

The straight razor with the handle parted after the rivet has been filed down.

Step 1

To remove the handle from the straight razor, simply file the end of the rivet flush with the razor handle. Pry the handle away from the tang using a screwdriver or similar flat piece of steel (Illus. 4-10).

The barber's straight razor is very sharp, so be careful when you are trying to remove the handle. One of the purposes of the handle was to allow the sharp edge of the blade to be folded into the handle. The handle protected the edge of the blade but it also prevented the barber from cutting himself when he was handling the razor before or after shaving. By removing this handle, you are also removing this original form of protection.

I suggest that you apply a few layers of masking tape over the edge of the blade. When folding the tape over the edge of the blade, do not fold the tape up to the sharp edge. Locate the fold in the tape away from the sharp edge approximately 1/16". In this way, there is a small buffer edge just in case you accidentally brush your fingers against the blade.

When you file the end of the rivet in order to remove the handle, the face of the handle will usually be marked by the file. If the handle is in perfect condition, you may want to save the handle, therefore you will not want these file marks on the face of the handle. To remove the rivet on the handle in this case, you can drill into the end of the rivet with a small drill bit. Stop the drill bit just as it enters the handle. The handle can now be parted in the manner already described at the start of this step.

Illus. 4-11

Cleaning the straight razor tang with emery cloth to improve the glue bond.

Step 2

Using emery cloth or sandpaper, clean the tang to remove the usual grimy film that has built up on the razor. This improves the glue bond (Illus. 4-11).

Do not place the blade of the straight razor in a steel jaw vise while trying to clean the tang. The straight razor, as I have already stated, is very hard and very brittle. Any pressure points on the blade, which are caused by the face of the steel jaws of the vise, may crack the blade. A piece of soft wood can be used on each face of the vise jaw to prevent the blade of the razor from breaking. The blade of the straight razor can now be held securely while you are cleaning the tang of the razor.

Illus. 4-12

Mark the matching faces of the pieces for the knife handle.

Step 3

Match one flat surface on each of the two pieces of wood and put a pencil mark on each face (Illus. 4-12). These surfaces must fit tightly against one another without any clamping at this time. If these surfaces are not flat, any stress that is developed when clamping the pieces of wood while glueing, could result in the handles eventually parting at the joint.

The use of a belt sander is one method of providing a flat surface on each piece of wood. However, these pieces of wood are very small and also very thin, and it would be dangerous to try to hold them on the fast moving belt. Unless you have many hours of experience on this machine, and you are very confident when using it, I advise you not to use this method to sand the faces of the wood.

The best and the safest method to sand the faces of the

wood, is to simply use a sheet of abrasive fastened to a flat board with the abrasive side facing up. It can be glued down flat or stapled at the four corners onto the board. Use a cloth or heavy paper backed abrasive such as emery cloth because it is more durable than regular sandpaper. The regular sandpaper tends to rip very easily and it also buckles when used in this instance. Now pass the piece of wood back and forth over the face of the abrasive cloth. Clamp the board to the top of the workbench to prevent the board from shifting as you are sanding the face of each piece of wood.

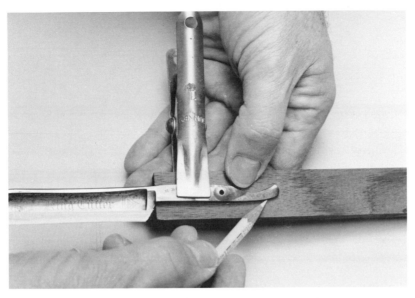

Illus. 4-13

The spring clamp is ideal for holding the tang in place while outlining
the tang on the wood.

Step 4

Place the tang of the razor on the marked face of one
piece of wood with the entire tang resting on the face of the wood.
The tang may be held in place with the finger tips, but a spring
clamp will hold the tang in place much more securely (Illus. 4-13).

Step 5

With a sharp pencil, trace the outline of the tang on the
face of the wood. Do not allow the tang to move while tracing the
outline. This outline is only traced on one piece of wood at this
time.

Illus. 4-14

Use the X-Acto knife with a No. 24 blade to cut down into the outline of the tang.

Step 6

Using the x-acto knife, score the outline of the tang into the face of the wood. Use light pressure on the initial cut. Repeat this cut around the outline to a depth of approximately 3/32″ (Illus. 4-14).

This particular step can result in some cut fingers or at least some very near cut fingers. The piece of wood is small and there is a tendency to try to hold the wood in place as you are cutting this outline near your fingers.

To add to this, there is a resistance to the tip of the x-acto knife blade while it is cutting this outline of the tang, which is developed in the hardwood itself. This resistance in the wood constantly changes the pressure that is required on the tip of the blade as you are making this cut. While outlining the tang, you must concentrate on the blade pressure at all times or the blade can slip off the line ever so quickly.

Cutting the tang outline around the end of the tang in a tight curve is another area where you must be extra careful because the blade can slip out of the cut and toward your fingers.

If you do cut yourself while making the carver's knife, it will most likely be while making these cuts for the outline of the tang. Once again, use light pressure on the x-acto blade and take these cuts down to the required depth in stages.

Illus. 4-15

Chiseling the recess for the razor tang. Note the jig or holding
device to hold the piece of wood in place.

Step 7

Using the 4 m.m. wide chisel, start to remove the wood in the outlined area of the tang. Use a little side to side rocking action with the edge of the chisel as you are chiseling out this recess. You may need to use the 2 m.m. wide chisel to remove the wood in the narrow areas of the recess.

A jig can be made to hold the piece of wood in place as you are chiseling out this recess. This holding device will help you to cut a better recess for the tang because with two hands on the chisel, there is more control when chiseling out the wood (Illus. 4-15).

The depth of the recess should be half of the thickness of the razor tang. There is a taper on the tang, so take care that you do not remove too much wood from the recess toward the end of the tang. Keep trying the tang in the recess until it fits as close as possible (Illus. 4-16).

Illus. 4-16

The recess completed in the piece of wood.

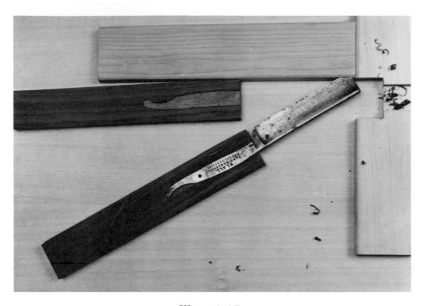

Illus. 4-17

The tang has been outlined on the second piece of wood and is
ready to be chiseled out.

Step 8

Place the other piece of wood on the bench with the
marked surface facing up. With the tang set into the recess of the
first piece, place both over the second piece of wood. Line up all of
the edges of the two pieces. Without moving the razor tang,
remove the first piece of wood which has already been recessed.
The razor must be firmly held in place while you are removing the
first piece of wood.

Now trace the outline of the tang onto the second piece
of wood (Illus. 4-17). If the tang moves, repeat this operation again
before tracing the outline of the tang onto the face of the wood.

Illus. 4-18

The tang is set into one recess and the other recess is completed.

Step 9

Now repeat steps 6 and 7. As you work on these steps, be sure to check the fit often between the two pieces of wood, with the tang set into the recess. Remove only enough wood from the recesses so that the two wood surfaces meet and there is no gap between them when assembled with the tang set in place. This step must be done with care — take your time. If the fit is sloppy, try again with two new pieces of wood (Illus. 4-18).

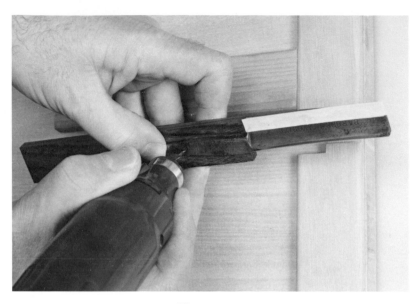

Illus. 4-19

Drilling through the hole in the tang and out the first piece of wood.

Step 10

To drill the hole for the nail rivet, select a drill bit which is the diameter of the nail. Do not drill the hole under size as this may result in splitting the wood handle when you are setting in the nail.

Place the tang into the recess of the first piece of wood. Now drill through the hole in the tang and out through the wood itself (Illus. 4-19). In this way, the hole is in perfect alignment with both the tang and the first piece of wood that forms the knife handle.

Assemble the tang into the recesses of the two pieces of wood. This time, drill through the hole that has already been drilled in the first piece, through the tang hole and out through the second piece of wood (Illus. 4-20).

Both the pieces of wood and the hole through the handle should now be perfectly aligned and matched.

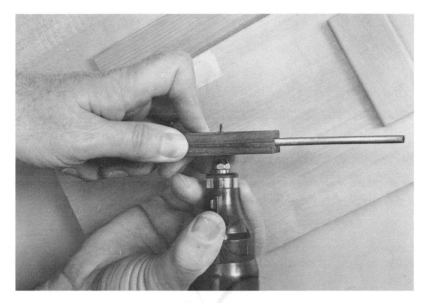

Illus. 4-20

Drilling through the second piece of wood to complete the hole for the rivet.

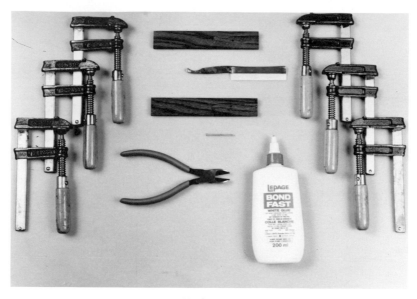

Illus. 4-21

Showing all the items necessary to glue the tang into the pieces of
wood that form the knife handle.

Step 11

The two pieces of wood and the tang are now ready for
glueing.

First try clamping the two wood pieces with the tang in
place, without any glue, to see where the clamps are best set on
the handle.

Lay out the straight razor and the pieces for the handle
on some newspaper, along with the clamps, the nail for the rivet,
the glue and the pliers (Illus. 4-21).

Spread the glue on both surfaces of the wood and also
into the recesses of the tang. Place the tang into one recess in the
handle. Set the second piece of wood over this assembly.
BEFORE APPLYING ANY CLAMPS, TWIST THE NAIL RIVET
INTO THE DRILLED HOLE USING THE PLIERS.

Apply the clamps with the razor pointing upward (Illus.4-22). This prevents the glue from running out of the handle. Use only enough pressure to close the joints in the wood. Do not overtighten the clamps. Prop up the handle with the razor pointing straight up after the excess glue has been removed from the outer edges. Do not remove the excess glue in the area where the razor enters the wood handle.

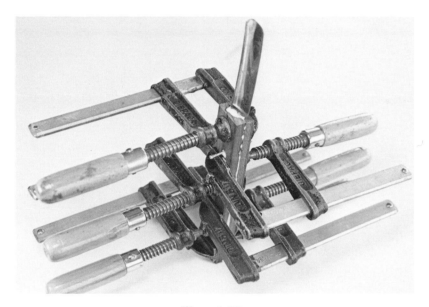

Illus. 4-22

The clamps are staggered on the handle. The blade is pointing straight up until the glue sets. The nail was inserted before the clamps were applied.

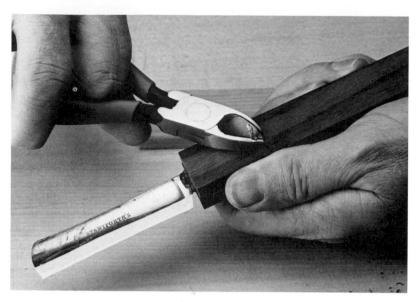

Illus. 4-23

The clamps have been removed and the nail rivet is ready to be cut
flush with the face of the wood.

Step 12

After 24 hours, you may remove the clamps (Illus. 4-23).
Using the side cutting pliers, cut the nail rivet as close to the faces
of the handle as possible. File the ends of the nail until they are
flush with the faces of the handle.

When using white glue, I let each knife sit for 3 days
before I begin to grind the knife. This waiting period ensures that
the glue has set properly in the handle.

Illus. 4-24

The blade is marked and is ready to be ground to its' proper length.
The recommended finished blade length is 2″ to 2⅛″.

Step 13

Most straight razors will have approximately 3″ of blade projecting from the wood handle at this stage.

I usually end up with a 2″ long blade on my finished carving knife. I would recommend this 2″ length of blade as the length of blade for your first knife (Illus. 4-24).

Because the steel is so hard in the straight razor, the only method which can be used to reduce the original length of the blade is to grind it off. A hacksaw cannot be used to cut the blade.

To shorten the blade, I use the corner of the grinding wheel on each face of the straight razor blade. This grinding forms a V shaped recess in the blade. When you have almost ground through, the end of the blade can be snapped off. It is advisable to wear some eye protection when you are snapping off the end of the blade just in case a small piece of steel breaks off and comes toward your face.

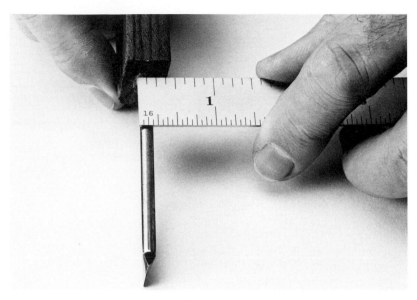

Illus. 4-25

This top view of the knife shows the thickness of the straight razor blade to be 3/16″ before we start grinding.

Step 14

We are now ready to grind the blade of the carver's knife. Remember that a straight razor is very hard and very brittle. The steel that is used to make a straight razor has the properties to provide an excellent knife for the wood carver. However, overheating and burning the steel will definitely render the blade useless to the carver.

Grind the blade very slowly and keep the blade cool by dipping it in cold water after every few seconds on the grinding wheel. The objective of the initial grinding is to remove the steel on each face of the blade at the top edge. This edge can measure 3/16″ thick on an average razor and this thickness must be reduced considerably (Illus. 4-25). There should be no trace of the razor being hollow ground when you have completed the grinding of the blade. Instead, it should be two flat faces which taper to the cutting edge. Grind both faces taking care to remove the same amount of steel from each face (Illus. 2-4). Grind the faces of the blade as flat as possible and avoid hollow grinding.

Now flatten the two faces, removing all grinding marks, using the coarse surface of the oil stone. Finish the faces of the blade on the fine surface of the oil stone. This step must be complete before the blade is shaped to suit the wood carver.

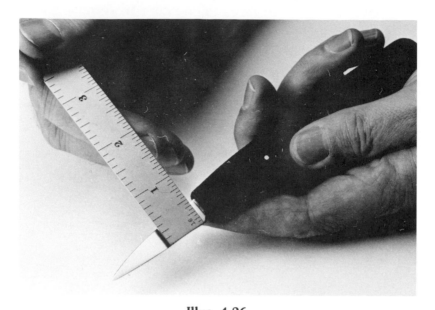

Illus. 4-26

The width of the blade is 7/16″ at the point where the blade meets the wood handle.

Step 15

The blade can now be ground to shape to suit the needs of each carver. I will usually start with a width of 7/16″ where the blade meets the wood handle (Illus. 4-26). From this widest part, the blade will taper to a point at the end of the blade. I have found that wide blades do not "roll" with the concave cut but instead, tend to dig into the wood.

As I have already mentioned, my blades will average between 2″ and 2⅛″ in length when finished. Of course the size of your carving will dictate the size of the blade for your knife. I find that the dimensions of my blades suit most carvers who have purchased my knives. They perform very well on average size carving projects.

When grinding the blade near the tip, you must use very little pressure on the grinding wheel. The tip of the blade will heat up very quickly and will burn if it is not kept cool. If the tip is burned, it will be necessary to grind this soft steel off. This will result in a shorter blade length so be careful from the start and regrinding a new tip will not be necessary.

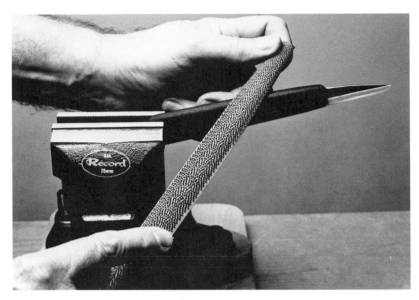

Illus. 4-27

The end of the wood handle is held in a vise while the handle is being shaped. Note the layers of masking tape on the sharp edge of the blade.

Step 16

The wood handle is now shaped to suit the wood carver. Some may disagree with my approach to knife making in that I shape my handles after I have finished grinding the blade. However, I find it easier to shape the handle to compliment the blade rather than shaping the blade to compliment the handle. You may wish to prove this theory for yourself with one knife. It is the end result that matters, whichever method that you decide to use.

A bench vise to grip the end of the handle, is a safe method for holding the knife while you are shaping the handle with the rasp (Illus. 4-27).

You may wish to apply layers of masking tape on the sharp edge of the blade, which will prevent you from cutting yourself while shaping the handle. Apply the masking tape as you did in step 1.

I prefer a slightly convex face on the sides of the handle with the top and bottom edges rounded. I have found that a round handle in section, similar to a broomstick, rotates in the carver's hand and causes more strain on the carver's hand. Round handled tools also tend to roll off the top of the workbench.

Shape your handles to suit your requirements, after all, they are your knives.

The amount of filing and sanding on the handle will depend on the finish that you will want on your knife. Avoid a highly polished handle because the polished surface will require more pressure on your grip than a rougher textured handle.

Illus. 4-28

A styrofoam block is used as a stand for the knife while the finish on the handle is drying.

Step 17

Some types of wood such as ebony and walnut will stain your hand if they are not sealed with a wood finish. The finish on the handle will not only prevent this bleeding of the wood color onto the palm of your hand, but will also bring out the grain and the color of the wood. The carver's knife is far more attractive with a finish on it, and it looks much more expensive than a knife that is not treated with a finish.

Apply one or two coats of urethane or lacquer if you wish to have a finish on your knife.

I use 2″ thick pieces of styrofoam board to act as a stand for my knife, while the finish on the handle is drying. Cut the 2″ thick boards into approximately 4″ squares. Locate the center of the 4″ square and push the pointed blade of the knife into the styrofoam block. Now you are able to hold the styrofoam block while you are applying the finish to the knife handle. When you have completed the brushing or spraying of the finish, the styrofoam block can be placed on the table top to support the knife in an upright position while it is drying (Illus. 4-28).

When the finish has completely dried, the knife is ready to be sharpened.

SHARPENING THE CARVER'S KNIFE

The merits of the rubberized abrasive wheel for chisel sharpening have been listed, and at first it would appear that this system should be used for knife sharpening also. Although there are carvers who use the wheel on their knife edges with success, I use and recommend the rubberized abrasive block.

The rubberized abrasive block is available in several sizes, with the 6″ × 2″ × ¼″ size being the least expensive for knife honing. The 6″ × 2″ face provides a large surface area for the back and forth stropping action that is required for knife sharpening. The block is also available in a 6″ × 2″ × 1″ size but, because of the extra thickness, this block is much more expensive. This is the size of block that I purchased ten years ago. The blocks are available in various grits, however, I use the extra fine grit for all of my knife honing.

The reason that I recommend the block for knife sharpening is that with the block, it is much easier to maintain the two flat faces of the knife blade which taper to the cutting edge. When using a wheel to hone the knife, there is a tendency to "roll" the edge of the blade. When this happens, the two faces must be flattened again on an oilstone.

When a rubberized abrasive block is new, it requires a "breaking in" period. The amount of use will determine the time required for "breaking in" the block. Several drops of oil can be rubbed into the surface of the block when you first purchase it. The oil provides a slick surface which speeds up the "breaking in" time. When it has penetrated the rubber surface, do not add any more oil. I always use my block dry, without oil or other lubricant.

The block is at its best when a black dust forms on the surface of the block where the honing is being performed. Do not wipe this dust off.

Remember that the block is a rubber material and can be cut, nicked or gouged. Be careful not to damage the honing surface.

When using the stropping action to hone the knife edge, the knife's cutting edge must trail on each stroke, and not lead on each stroke (Illus. 5-1). Although this may seem quite obvious, some wood carvers have forgotten this rule, and have cut the surface of their blocks.

To start the honing of the knife blade, place the blade of the knife flat on the rubberized abrasive block. If you are right handed, place the forefinger of your left hand on the flat blade

Illus. 5-1

The knife blade is set on the rubberized abrasive block. The edge of the blade is trailing for the direction of the stroke as indicated by the arrow.

Illus. 5-2

The forefinger is placed on the blade to exert more pressure while honing.

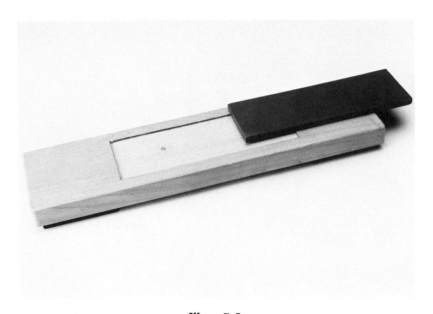

Illus. 5-3

Showing the recess in the wood block for the rubberized abrasive block.

surface (Illus. 5-2). This is the finger that will exert most of the pressure on the blade while pushing it forward and drawing it back on the block. The right hand grips the handle and moves the knife back and forth. Avoid too much downward pressure on the handle of the knife because this will cause a strain on the blade at the point where it meets the wood handle. If you push down on the handle too hard, to gain more blade pressure against the rubberized abrasive block, the blade may eventually break. This additional pressure on the handle causes the blade to flex and eventually break because of metal fatigue.

You must concentrate on not letting your left forefinger slip off the blade when drawing the blade back and pushing it forward. Practice with light finger pressure on the blade until you have established a rhythm for this sharpening technique. Build this finger pressure up to the point where you feel comfortable while stropping back and forth. Remember that the more pressure that you exert with your forefinger, the faster the sharpening time.

Hold the face of the knife blade flat on the surface of the block when stropping back and forth. In this way, you are maintaining the flat tapered surface leading to the knife edge. There is the temptation to lift the back edge slightly, which in turn hones the cutting edge faster. This results in the edge "rolling" and over the long run will mean more work because the two faces of the blade must be flattened again on a stone.

When carving, hone the blade often to maintain a sharp edge. Don't let it get dull and then try rehoning the edge.

The rubber block can be glued, using white glue, to a 2" wide × ¾" thick × 12" long board. If you glue the block in the center of the 12" length, this will provide 3 inches of board at each end for C clamping to the edge of your workbench. The ¼" thick rubber block can also be recessed approximately ⅛" into a wood block similar to the oilstone block (Illus. 5-3). The advantage of recessing the rubber block into the wood, is that the rubber block can be flipped over, thus providing two honing surfaces. If you purchase the 6" × 2" × 1" abrasive block, as I have done, then you would recess it ½" into the wood. In this case, the rubber block will look identical to an oilstone at first glance. I must point out to spectators at carving shows that I am, in fact, using a rubberized abrasive block and not an oilstone. They do look alike, especially when the rubberized abrasive block has been used for a few months.

A carver can expect to have this relatively inexpensive block for many years. I have used my rubberized abrasive block for ten years and it shows very little sign of wear. It is also nice to know that, should you accidentally drop it on a hard floor surface, it will not break as would the expensive oil or waterstones.

CARVING TEMPLATES

I have drawn the patterns for the two sizes of the boot as shown in Illus. 6-1 and 6-2. Both patterns are full size and are identical in size to my carvings of these boots. Over the years they have simply become known as the small boot and the large boot. I will be using these two descriptions of size in the following chapters of this book to refer to either boot.

The small boot carving blank is cut from material which is $2\frac{1}{8}''$ thick while the large boot carving blank is cut from material which is $2\frac{7}{8}''$ thick. The face dimensions of each boot can be obtained from the patterns. I have purposely not given the face dimensions of each boot because these dimensions will depend on how much material allowance each wood carver leaves for bandsawing, and also on his or her approach to bandsawing the carving blank.

If you intend to bandsaw just one or two carving blanks, I suggest that you first trace the pattern of the boot on a piece of tracing paper and then transfer it onto the wood using carbon paper. If you intend to bandsaw a number of boot blanks, I would advise you to make a more permanent template.

I use flexible white plastic sheets which I purchase from a specialty shop that deals in plastics, for my template material (Illus. 6-3). This plastic can be bought in various size sheets and is approximately 1/16″ thick. I particularly like this plastic because you can trace on it using a pencil, it can be shaped easily with a knife, and it is not brittle and can be bent to follow a curvature in the wood. The pattern for the sole of the boot is a good example of where a flexible material is required, because this surface is curved.

After you have traced the boot pattern on the white plastic, it can be cut to shape with a knife in very little time (Illus. 6-4). The material is quite soft and does not dull a knife at all. In fact, I use my carving knives on this plastic. Normally my carving knives are used on nothing else but my carvings, but this plastic is the only exception.

With this plastic template, it is very simple and very quick to trace this pattern on the wood for as many carving blanks as you need.

I personally hate to trace a pattern on tracing paper and then transfer it on the wood with carbon paper. I find that the tracing paper is usually damaged by the pencil point when you are transferring the pattern onto the wood. The accuracy of the paper pattern is lost as a result, if the pattern is used too often. This method of transferring a pattern on the wood is fine if it is only used for a few carvings and then the traced out pattern is thrown away.

The plastic template is so handy when you decide to carve that particular subject at some time in the future. I always write the stock thickness required for each particular carving on the back face of each plastic template. I then drill a hole in the template so that I may hang it up on a nail or hook. Whenever I want to carve a specific subject, I simply remove the template from the hook, check the material thickness on the reverse side and trace the outline on the wood in seconds. It is at that time that I appreciate the little time that I had spent to cut the plastic template.

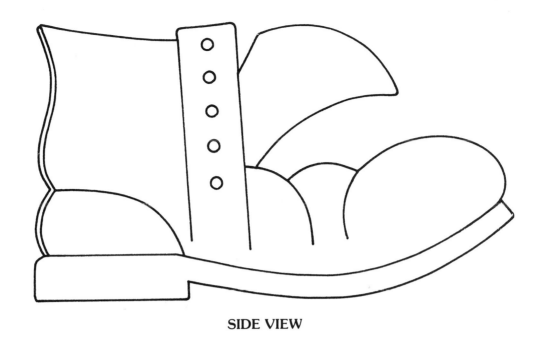

SIDE VIEW

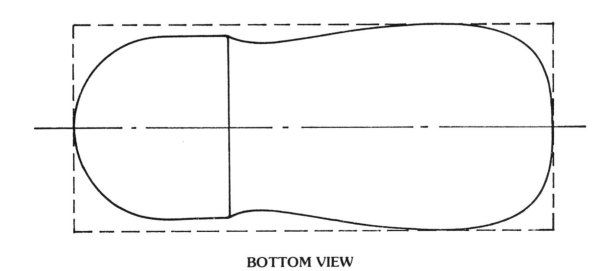

BOTTOM VIEW

ILLUS. 6-1

Full size pattern for the small boot.

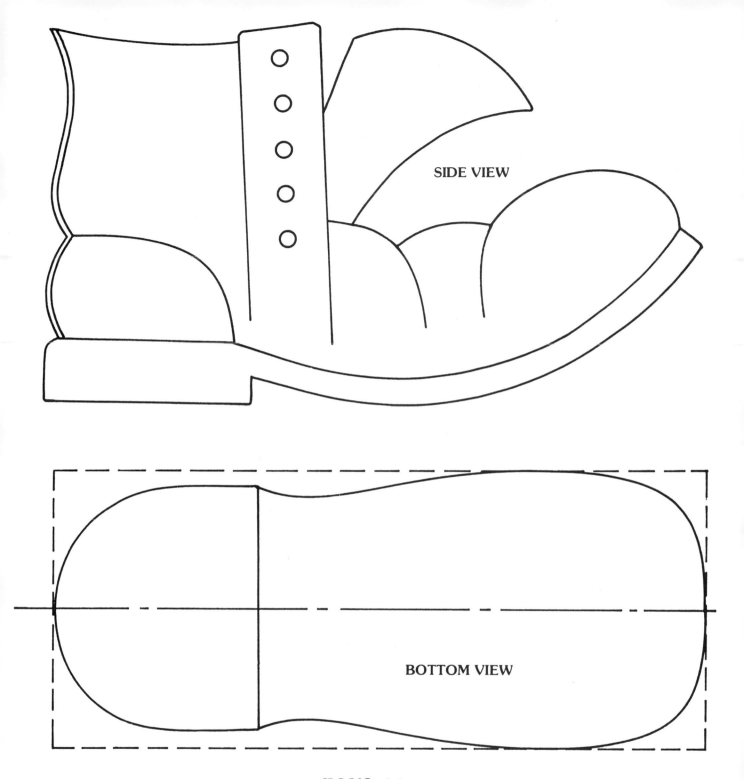

SIDE VIEW

BOTTOM VIEW

ILLUS. 6-2

Full size pattern for the large boot.

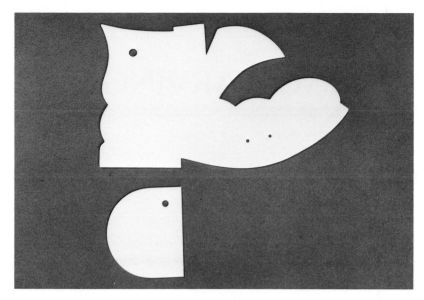

Illus. 6-3

Plastic templates for the small boot and the heel. Two holes are used to hang the templates on a hook or nail. The other two holes indicate the start of the crease lines on the toe area of the boot.

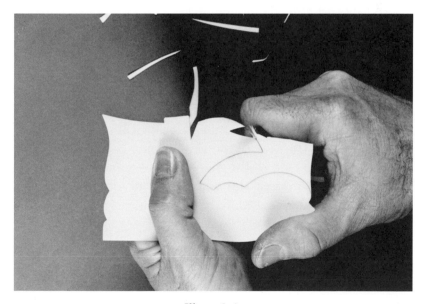

Illus. 6-4

The plastic used for the templates can be cut with the carver's knife.

CUTTING CARVING BLANKS

I have already mentioned in the chapter Making The Carver's Knife, that the grinder unit and the bandsaw are the two pieces of machinery that I cannot do without. There are books for wood carving on the market that suggest that handsaws such as a coping saw or a bow saw can be used to cut a wood carving blank. I consider these suggested alternatives to the bandsaw for cutting carving blanks, to be unfair to the wood carver. As a boy, I used a coping saw for many woodworking projects, and to this day, I still own one. I would like to think that I am as proficient with these handsaws as the average woodworker. However, I would not consider trying to cut a carving blank on any other saw but the bandsaw.

It is virtually impossible to cut these boot blanks accurately with any type of handsaw. The material for the boot blanks being $2\frac{1}{8}$" or $2\frac{7}{8}$" thick, makes it difficult to cut the carving blanks square with the face of the sides. If any carving blank is not cut square with the face of the sides, it presents problems to the professional wood carver, let alone the novice wood carver. Cutting the carving blank square with the face of the sides is most important (Illus. 7-2).

If the bandsaw is set up correctly, each cut will be guaranteed to be square with the face of the carving blank. The bandsaw will also allow you to cut the carving blank in far less time than if you were to use any of the handsaws.

If you do not have a bandsaw, I suggest that you find a woodworking shop that will allow you to cut your carving blanks or have someone in the shop cut them for you for a nominal charge.

I use a ¼″ wide blade to cut the boot blank because this blade width provides a tighter turning or cutting radius than a wider blade. The curved lines on the carving blanks can easily be followed using a ¼″ wide bandsaw blade.

When I am cutting a carving blank, I make a point of leaving the pencil line on the wood. I cut on the outside of the pencil line which allows for the roughness left on the face of the wood by the bandsaw blade. This is more critical on small carvings, but this approach to bandsawing has become the standard way for me.

To prepare the piece of wood for drilling and bandsawing, we must check that the bottom face is planed flat and that the faces of the two sides are square with the bottom face.

Before we proceed to bandsaw the carving blank, we must first drill a hole starting from the top face of the wood block and into the block itself. The boot can be carved without the aid of this hole but the carving would take much more time to complete. Not only is a lot of excess wood removed quickly, but the hole provides a cavity for the wood to curl into when you are chiseling out the interior of the boot. The advantage of this drilled hole will become evident when you reach this point in the actual carving of the boot.

I use a ⅞″ diameter Forstner drill bit for the hole in the small boot and a 1⅜″ diameter Forstner drill bit for the hole in the large boot (Illus. 7-3).

I have indicated the location of the center line and the depth of the hole on the bandsaw cutting sequence drawing (Illus. 7-1). The location and the depth of the hole for the small and the large boot would be proportional to these dimensions.

The use of a drill press would simplify the drilling of this hole because the depth guage on the drill press can be set to the bottom limit of the hole. The drilled hole will also be at right angles to the bottom face of the boot if the drill press table is set up properly.

When drilling a hole to these depths with a Forstner drill bit, I drill the hole in stages to avoid clogging the drill bit. Drill into the wood until you feel the drill bit start to clog. Stop drilling the hole and bring the drill bit up and out of the block of wood. Knock out the excess wood from the partially drilled hole and proceed to drill the hole again. Repeat this sequence as many times as is necessary to reach the bottom of the hole.

We are now ready to begin bandsawing the boot. This is how I proceed to cut a boot blank using the bandsaw. I have indicated a number in a circle to put the bandsaw cuts in a numerical sequence. The arrow on the circle indicates the direction of the cut.

The bottom edge of the heel does not have a cut number because the plastic template is set flush with the edge of the bottom face when you are tracing the outline of the boot on the wood. In this way, the heel does not have a bandsaw cut surface, but instead is smooth and flat.

When making long saw cuts that must be backed out of the block of wood, for example cut numbers 13 and 19, it is advisable to stop the bandsaw at the end of the cut while the blade is still in the block. With the saw at a full stop, gently guide the block of wood back out without pulling on the blade. If you try to back out the blade with the bandsaw still operating, you risk the chance of pulling the blade off the drive wheels. If this does happen, the blade must be installed all over again, which involves setting up the guides etc. Stopping the bandsaw as suggested, will save a lot of time and cursing in the long run.

After cut numbers 19 and 20 are made, a wedged shaped piece of wood will remain in this area. Stop the bandsaw at the end of cut number 20 and then remove this wedge shaped piece of wood.

When all the 20 cuts are completed, there will be a little wood to remove in the area between points A, B and C. This is done by a series of short bandsaw cuts, numbered 21, ending each time at the pencil line.

Your carving blank is now ready to have the necessary guidelines drawn onto it (Illus. 7-4).

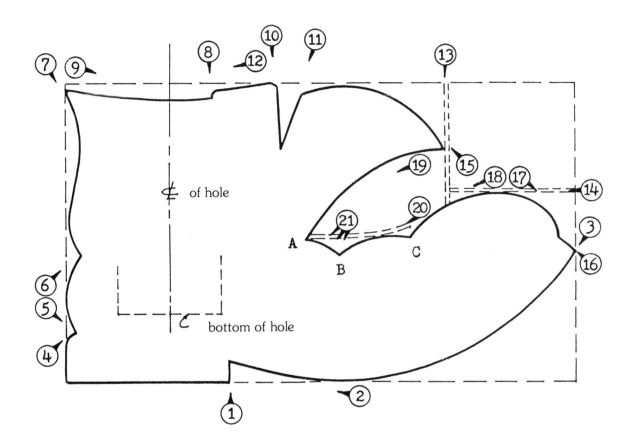

ILLUS. 7-1

The sequence for bandsawing
the boot carving blank.

NOTE: Drawing not full size.

Illus. 7-2

A carving blank must be cut square with its face.

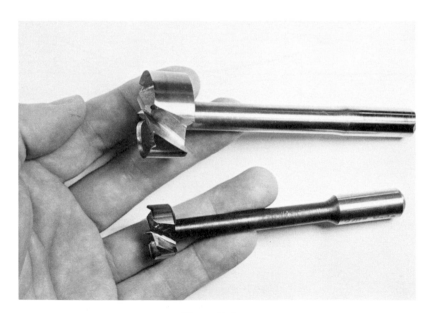

Illus. 7-3

A Forstner drill bit is used to remove the excess wood from the interior of the boot.

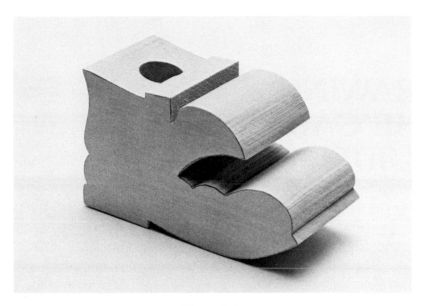

Illus. 7-4

The boot carving blank which has been drilled and bandsawed, is
ready to have the necessary guidelines drawn on it.

DRAWING THE CARVING GUIDELINES

The guidelines which are shown as dark lines in Illus. 8-1, are the basic guidelines that are necessary for the front and the top views of the carving blank.

Refer to the patterns of the boots in Illus. 6-1 and 6-2 for the shape of the heel and the sole. The heel pattern may be drawn on the bottom face of the carving blank according to the actual shape shown (Illus. 8-2).

The patterns of the soles as shown on the bottom views are not the true length. An allowance must be made for the curved surface of the sole. To establish the true length of the sole, you could step off this true length from the front view using a pair of dividers. You could also bend a piece of white plastic over the curved surface of the sole after you have bandsawed the carving blank, and then mark the true length with a pencil. Now it is just a matter of altering the sole pattern to suit this true length. Be sure to start the piece of plastic at the junction of the heel and the sole and then bend the plastic over to the toe.

I personally do not use a pattern for the toe and for the tongue of the boot. In these instances, the natural flow of the curve is dictated by the width of the boot blank itself.

A center line which may be drawn around the carving blank, is a great help for the wood carver (Illus. 8-3). It helps to maintain symmetry on the carving, although for this boot, you may feel that symmetry is not desirable. After all, it is a form of

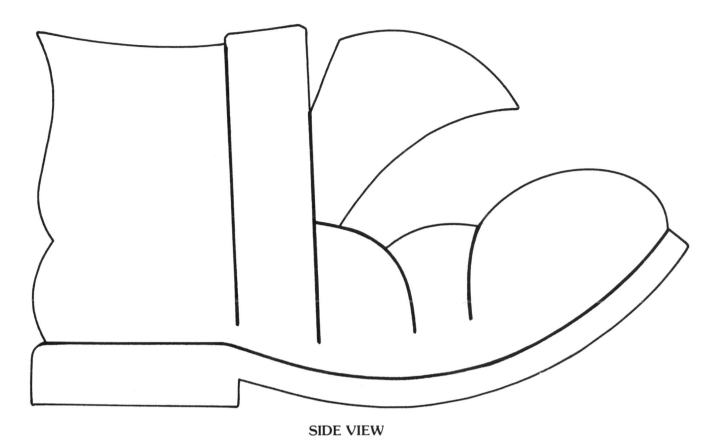

SIDE VIEW

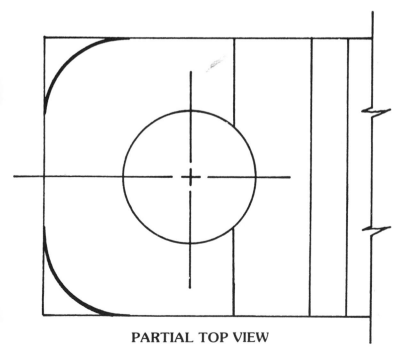

PARTIAL TOP VIEW

ILLUS. 8-1
Guideline layout for the large boot.

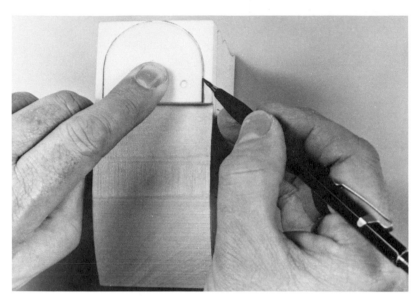

Illus. 8-2

Tracing the heel pattern on the boot blank.

Illus. 8-3

The boot blank with all the guidelines drawn on it.

caricature carving and a boot should not look too perfect. The center line may be used however, to indicate just how far that you are actually moving away from a truly symmetrical carving.

Reading the preceeding chapters and preparing the boot blank must have made it seem that the time of actual wood carving would never arrive. If you have made or have purchased a good carving knife, and have attained a degree of proficiency in the sharpening of knives and chisels, you are ready for the actual carving of the boot.

CARVING THE BOOT

Illus. 9-1

Small boot completely carved, with lace holes drilled,
and ready for staining.

TOOLS REQUIRED TO CARVE THE SMALL BOOT:

1) A carver's knife with a blade length of approximately 2".
2) A carver's knife with a blade length of approximately 1". An x-acto knife with a No. 24 sharp pointed blade can be used as a substitute.
3) No. 3 gouge - 8 m.m. wide
4) No. 5 gouge - 16 m.m. wide
5) No. 7 gouge - 14 m.m. wide
6) No. 3 spoon gouge - 8 m.m. wide
7) 4 m.m. straight chisel
8) 8 m.m. straight chisel
9) 12 m.m. straight chisel
10) 12 m.m. skew cut chisel
11) Sharpening equipment

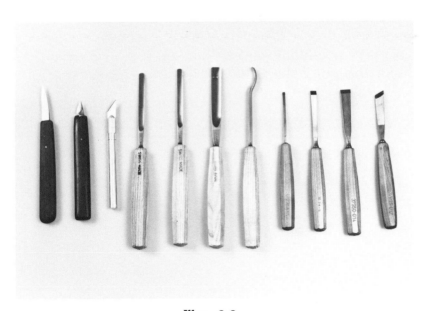

Illus. 9-2

Tools used to carve the small boot.

Step 1

You begin the small boot carving by making a vertical cut along the entire length of the guideline for the heel and the sole.

Start with a depth of cut that you feel you will be able to control. Do not let the knife slip off the pencil line as you make this cut. Remember that accidental knife and chisel cuts or other marks of any kind may show up on your finished carving. I like to refer to these accidental cuts as overcuts. I will be using this term often in this chapter to point out areas on the carving, where overcuts can affect the appearance of your completed carving.

The vertical cut should be worked down to a depth of approximately 3/16″. It will vary in depth as you proceed to carve the heel and the sole of the boot, but we will start with 3/16″.

I use a short blade knife to make this vertical cut because there is the chance of breaking the tip of the blade if a long and pointed blade is used. If you have made just one carver's knife and the blade is pointed, I suggest that you use a very sharp x-acto knife for this cut instead.

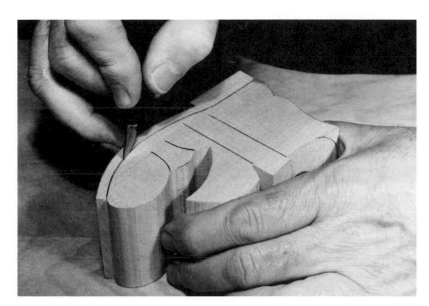

Illus. 9-3

Step 1 in progress.

Step 2

Side cut into these vertical cuts using a short blade knife. The angle of these side cuts is approximately 45 degrees. Work these cuts down gradually to a depth of 3/16" - do not try to remove a lot of wood using one deep cut.

Avoid overcutting past the vertical cut line because these overcut marks will show on the finished edge of the heel and sole.

This combination of the side cut and the vertical cut is used up to and including step 6.

It is important when you are carving, that you always feel comfortable in the fact that the carving blank is being held securely. Try to have the best possible grip on the carving as you start each new step. Usually the most comfortable grip is also the safest way to hold the carving blank, but this is not always the case. Take a moment to study the direction of each knife and chisel cut and then decide on the best way to hold your carving to avoid any cut fingers.

For this step, you will notice that the second finger of my left hand is set in the space between the tongue and the boot. The forefinger pushes down on the blade of the knife as you are making these cuts. The thumb fits comfortably in the curved area at the back of the boot. In this way, the thumb and second finger prevent the lateral movement of the carving blank and keep the carving blank from slipping on the workbench.

Illus. 9-4

Step 2 in progress.

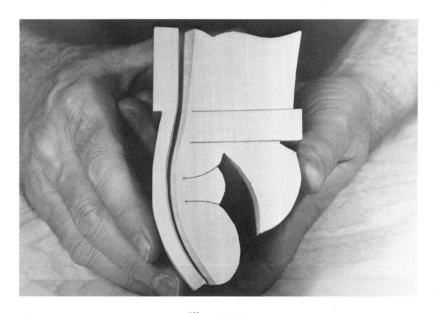

Illus. 9-5

Step 2 completed.

Step 3

Using the carver's knife, the two sides of the heel are trimmed down to the proper width. Use the guidelines that were drawn on the bottom view of the heel to establish this width.

When trimming the heel to the proper width, start your knife cut approximately ½″ beyond the square corner of the heel. The direction of these cuts will be toward the back of the boot. Do not start at the back of the boot, with the cuts being made toward the sole.

You will find it necessary to use two different types of knife cuts to complete this step. On one side of the heel, use the pull cut in which the blade of the knife is being drawn toward the thumb. On the other side of the heel, you will be using the push cut in which the blade is being pushed away from you with the thumb of the opposite hand.

Always be careful that the tip of the knife blade is not accidentally cutting into the side of the boot.

The side cut and the vertical cut may have to be used again to increase the depth of the groove that was cut in step 2.

Illus. 9-6

Step 3 in progress.

Illus. 9-7

Step 3 completed.

Step 4

The curved portion at the back of the heel is now rounded off.

To begin this step, you must continue the groove that was made in step 2 around the back of the boot. The vertical cut from step 1 is carried around the back of the boot along with the side cut from step 2. As you work toward the center line at the back of the boot, the groove will taper off in depth. This groove will appear very deep at the corners at this stage, because the back of the boot has not been rounded off as yet.

To cut the curved line on the heel, you start by setting the carving blank on the workbench with the bottom surface of the heel and sole facing up. Trim the heel to the guideline that you have drawn on the bottom face, using the push cut with the carver's knife. The forefinger of the left hand will be used to push the blade into the wood and not the thumb of the left hand as was the case in step 3. The thumb will be used, along with the second, third and fourth fingers of your left hand, to hold the carving blank in place as you are trimming down this curved area.

Try to carve the edge of the heel as square as possible to the bottom face of the boot.

Remember not to overcut into the body of the boot.

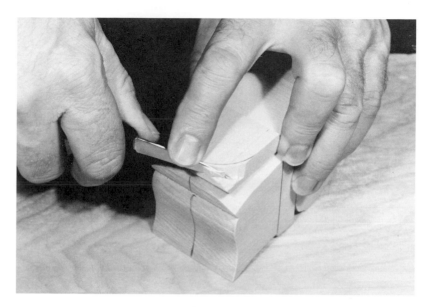

Illus. 9-8

Step 4 in progress.

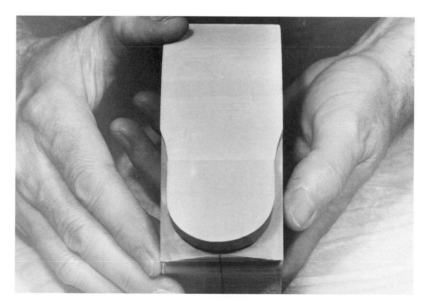

Illus. 9-9

Step 4 completed.

Step 5

Shape the narrowest parts of the sole which are located near the square corners of the heel. Because of the grain of the wood in this concave curved portion, it will be necessary to cut in both directions in order to reach the narrowest point of the sole. This is one area where a very sharp knife is needed. In order to cut in these two directions and to have these cuts meet at the low point of this concave curve, the knife must be very sharp. It is also an ideal location on a carving to judge the skill of the woodcarver. I look at areas, similar to these when judging a carving, to see if the use of sandpaper was necessary to eliminate the final knife marks.

Proceed by carving the sole outline to its' widest point. At this widest point, the round front or toe area of the sole will begin. The vertical cut and the side cut in steps 1 and 2 must be used again to follow the outline of the sole.

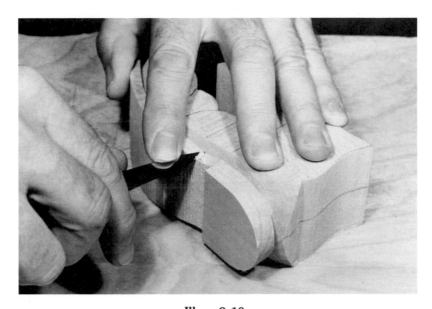

Illus. 9-10

Step 5 in progress.

Illus. 9-11

Step 5 completed.

Step 6

Shaping the toe area of the sole is similar to the procedure for carving the heel. It is a combination of the vertical cut in step 1, the side cut in step 2 and the rounding of the curved area of the heel as described in step 4.

The pull cut toward the thumb of the hand that is holding the knife, and the push cut, which uses the pushing action of the forefinger of the opposite hand, are both used for the toe area.

Be especially careful that you do not overcut into the toe of the boot. It is very easy to accidentally cut or mark the toe while you are shaping the sole, and this is one area of the boot where marks would be noticeable on the finished carving. You may not notice these overcut marks now, but they will appear when the stain and the finish is applied to the boot.

The prospective buyer always seems to inspect the toe area of the boot before he or she decides to purchase the carving, and these marks could discourage them from buying your carving.

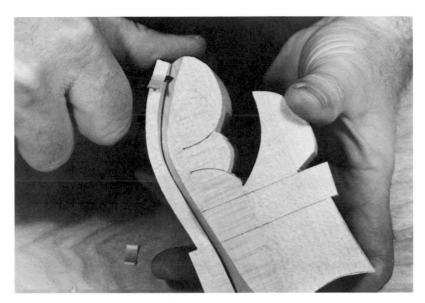

Illus. 9-12

Step 6 in progress.

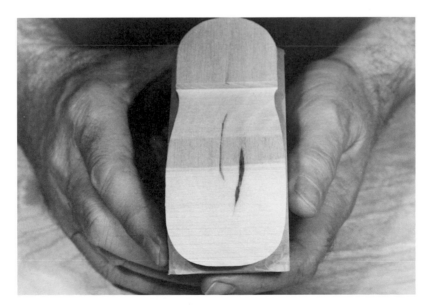

Illus. 9-13

Step 6 completed.

Step 7

The two round corners at the back of the carving blank are shaped next. These round corners should have been drawn on the top view of the carving blank according to Illus. 8-1. Use a radius of ¾" for the round corners on the small boot.

Place the boot on the workbench with the heel and the sole facing down.

You will be making a vertical cut with the carver's knife at both corners. Use the forefinger of the left hand to push on the knife blade as you make these cuts. The thumb and the remaining fingers of your left hand are used to hold the boot blank securely while you are cutting these corners. Continue these vertical cuts down approximately ¾". Work these cuts to the pencil guideline but do not cut away the pencil line.

Do not attempt to round the back face of the boot at the same time that you are making these vertical cuts. This will be your next step.

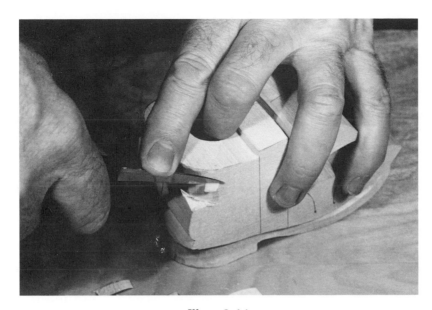

Illus. 9-14

Step 7 in progress.

Illus. 9-15

Step 7 completed.

Step 8

   In step 15 of Making a Carver's Knife I discussed blade widths and the demands of the concave or "roll" cut on the knife blade. This is our first encounter with this cut. Using the rounded corners which you have just shaped as your boot outline, you start to shape the upper half of the back of the boot. Start at the top of the boot and carry this rolling cut downwards in the direction of the heel. This direction of the cut applies to one side only. The other side of the boot will have the cut rolling toward the top of the boot. To make the roll cut, draw the blade of the knife into the wood and then roll it out toward the end of the cut. Make this cutting action as smooth as you possibly can.

   There will be an area in the center of the back of the boot that will be left uncarved at this time.

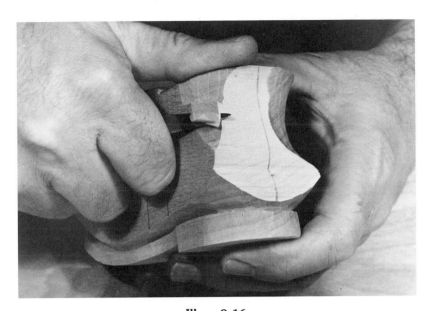

Illus. 9-16

Step 8 in progress.

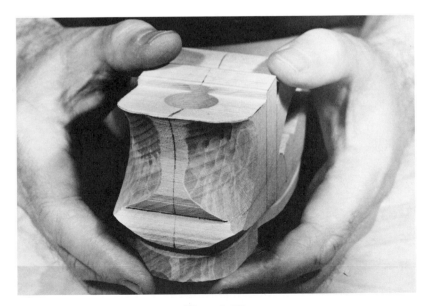

Illus. 9-17

Step 8 completed.

Step 9

Round the boot just below the area completed in step 8. Blend these cuts into the side cuts made in conjunction with the heel in step 4. As in step 8, there will be an area in the center of the back of the boot that will be left uncarved at this time. When this is completed, start with the tip of your finger at the top edge of the boot, and run it down to the heel. There should be a smooth and continuous curve from start to finish. Remove any high spots that interrupt the natural flow of the curve.

Use small cuts when working on a carving of this size. The texture created by the knife cuts should compliment the size of the carving.

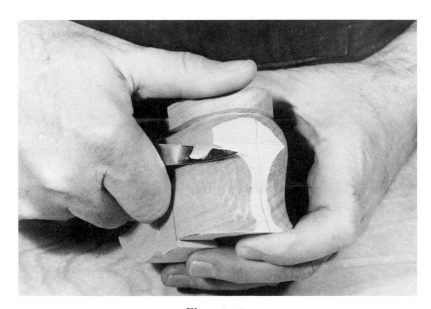

Illus. 9-18

Step 9 in progress.

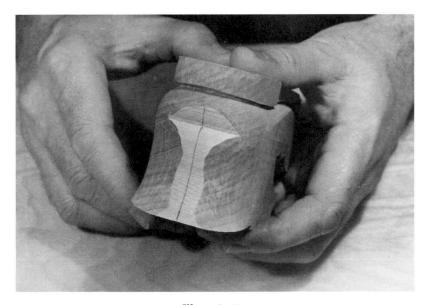

Illus. 9-19

Step 9 completed.

Step 10

The next step in carving the boot, is to round the front of the tongue. This curved part of the tongue determines its general shape, so you should inspect the tongue after each cut when you feel that you are nearing the final shape. If you remove too much wood and then find that you are not satisfied with the shape of the tongue, you must cut the curve down until it is right. This additional cutting of the curve at the front of the tongue will affect the overall appearance of the boot, so take your time. The shape of the finished curve should be pleasing to the eye and should not have a pointed look to it. Look straight down at the tongue when judging whether this curved outline is acceptable or not.

I do not use pencil guidelines to outline the shape of the tongue because it is awkward to trace a pattern on this very short and very curved surface. As I have mentioned in the chapter for Drawing The Carving Guidelines, the natural flow of this curve is dictated by the width of the boot blank itself.

This curved top view outline will be cut in the same way that you shaped the two round corners at the back of the boot in step 7. These are vertical cuts and will be cut down in the direction of the workbench. Use the forefinger of the left hand to push down on the blade of the knife.

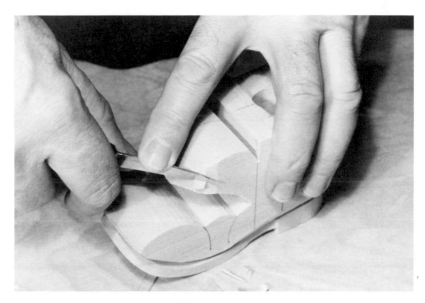

Illus. 9-20

Step 10 in progress.

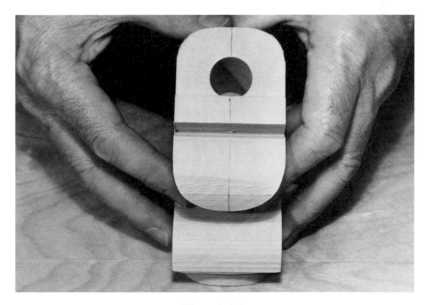

Illus. 9-21

Step 10 completed.

Step 11

Some of the excess wood on the underside of the tongue is removed in this step. These are not the finished cuts on the tongue. The only reason for removing this excess wood at this time, is to allow the wood carver easier access to the toe area.

Hold the boot blank as shown, and roll cut toward the curved outline which you have just completed in the previous step. Use the pull cut and the push cut for the appropriate faces of the tongue. When using the pull cut, the boot blank is held in your left hand. When using the push cut on the opposite side of the tongue, the boot blank will be set on its side on the workbench.

Throughout my book, I do not indicate the side of the carving that corresponds to the pull or push cut, because selecting the proper cut for each side of the boot will be obvious to the wood carver.

The roll cut is the most basic of knife cuts, but it can also be the most impressive to the spectator. If you wish to demonstrate just how sharp your carving knives really are, this is the cut that you would use. I would like to think of the roll cut as the most graceful knife cut that a wood carver can use, assuming that his or her knives are sharp of course.

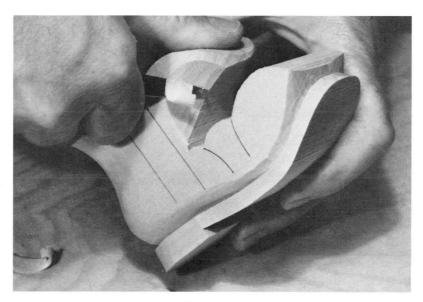

Illus. 9-22

Step 11 in progress.

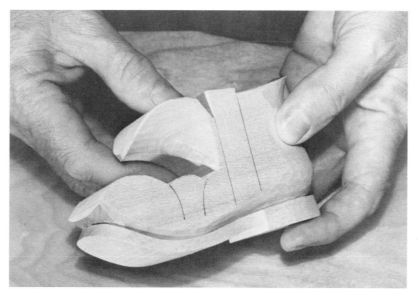

Illus. 9-23

Step 11 completed.

Step 12

  You are ready to shape the toe and the front part of the boot. Start by making V shaped cuts on the four guidelines which represent the creases in the toe area. These guidelines are shown on the side view of the boot in Illus. 8-1.

  Use the four guidelines as the centers of these V shaped grooves. The V shaped groove will stop $\frac{3}{8}$″ short of the line of the sole. The depth of the groove will be reduced as it approaches the line of the sole and the groove should blend into the side of the boot.

  When complete, the bottom point of each V shaped cut should start on one side of the boot and proceed around to the other side. This crease line should be a smooth curved line that is symmetrical on the toe of the boot.

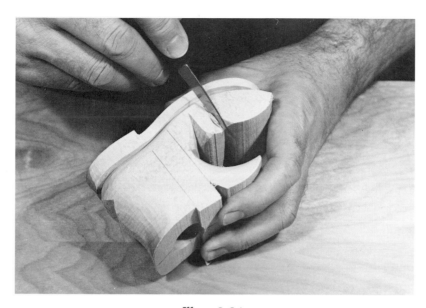

Illus. 9-24

Step 12 in progress.

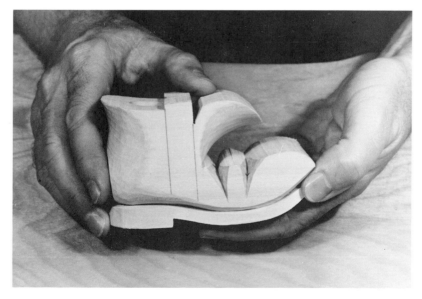

Illus. 9-25

Step 12 completed.

Step 13

The toe of the boot is now rounded to its final shape. It is a combination of knife cuts toward the front of the boot and toward the V shaped cuts which were completed in the previous step.

Rough out the shape of the toe by carving the high points down first. The curvature of toe should be similar to the curvature of the crease lines that were cut in the previous step. With the general shape of the toe now established, use the smaller knife cuts to arrive at the finished shape of the toe.

Be careful when carving near the sole of the boot. Watch that the tip of the knife blade does not overcut into the edge of the sole. As I have mentioned, the toe area seems to be one of the places on the boot that people first look at, so try to make the shape of the toe and the finished cuts as good as you possibly can.

Be critical of your own work — keep carving the toe until you are totally happy with its shape and with the final texture that has resulted from the knife cuts.

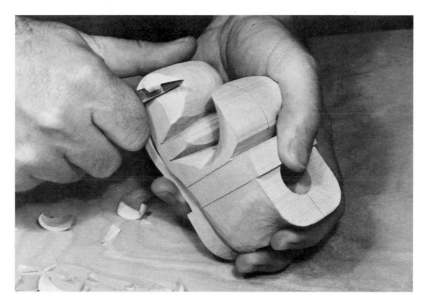

Illus. 9-26

Step 13 in progress.

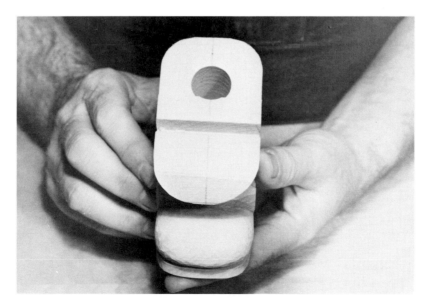

Illus. 9-27

Step 13 completed.

Step 14

The raised portion between the toe and the tongue is shaped next. As in the previous step, start by cutting down the high points to arrive at a flat surface that will follow the curvature already established by the toe and the crease lines from step 12. Using this flat surface as your reference point, this raised area is now rounded off with a series of small knife cuts.

Both the pull and the push cut with the knife will be used to complete this area of the carving.

You will be cutting in the direction of the finished toe for half of this raised area, so you must be careful to control the knife blade at the end of each cut. Do not overcut into the finished faces of the toe or the sole.

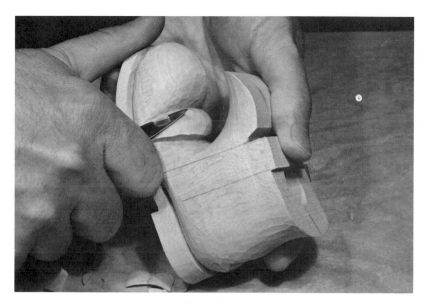

Illus. 9-28

Step 14 in progress.

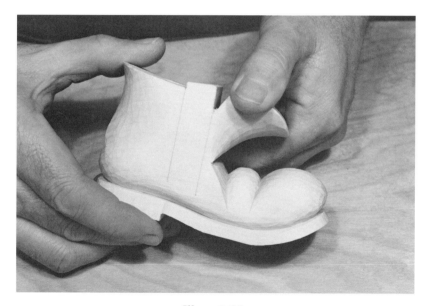

Illus. 9-29

Step 14 completed.

Step 15

       With the boot sitting on its side, you make a vertical cut on the first line of the lace hole area. It is very difficult to state the depth of this cut because it does vary in depth. It follows the sloping contour of the tongue and also follows the body of the boot down to the sole. See Illus. 9-36. This vertical cut is very shallow at the point where this lace hole portion meets the curved surface of the body of the boot. The vertical cuts above this area, which are in line with the tongue, can be ¼″ deep to start. You should use the x-acto knife for these cuts as you did in Step 1.

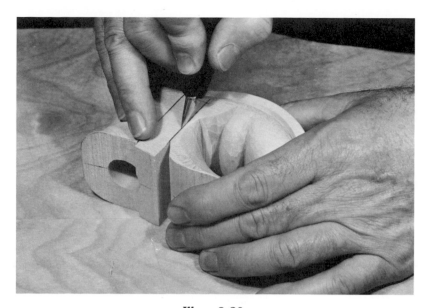

Illus. 9-30

Step 15 in progress.

Step 16

You are at the point in your carving where a chisel is first used. Using an 8 m.m. or 12 m.m. straight chisel, you start to shape the sides of the tongue. Work to the vertical cut lines completed in the previous step. Start at the curved outline of the tongue and proceed to chisel the tongue to the point where the tongue meets the boot. The width across the tongue at the point where it meets the boot is 1⅛". The vertical cuts from the previous step will be cut deeper in order to meet the chisel cuts on the tongue. You will not complete the entire face of the tongue with the chisel. This is the next step. Do not overcut the vertical cuts into the curved surface of the tongue.

Illus. 9-31

Step 16 in progress.

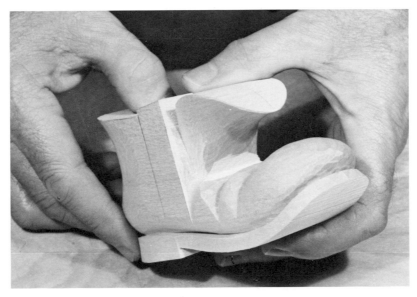

Illus. 9-32

Step 16 completed.

Step 17

Using the carver's knife, you complete the underside of the tongue next. The pull cut and the push cut are both started at the intersection of the tongue and the boot. Work these cuts to the curved outline of the tongue as established in step 10.

The finished cuts on the underside of the tongue should be a series of smooth and flowing cuts. They should not be short and abruptly changing cuts that interrupt the graceful lines of this surface of the boot.

Avoid marking the finished areas on the toe with the back edge of the knife as you are carving in this confined space.

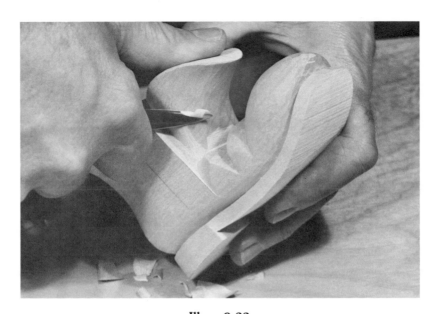

Illus. 9-33

Step 17 in progress.

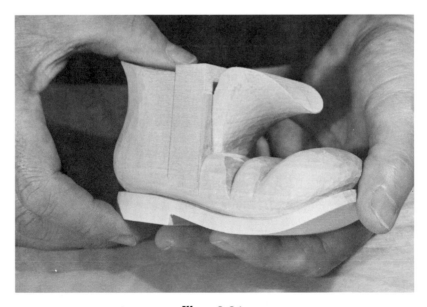

Illus. 9-34

Step 17 completed.

Step 18

The area of the boot located below the tongue is completed next. This is an area of the boot where you are carving in several directions, with the grain of the wood dictating the direction for each cut. You will be cutting toward the intersection of the tongue and the boot, toward the crease line behind the toe area, toward the vertical cut that was made in step 15 and also toward the sole of the boot.

Starting at the point where the tongue meets the boot, round off this area up to the crease line. Shape the area to the sole and to the vertical cut next.

Just another reminder to avoid overcutting into the many finished surfaces that are now on the boot.

Keep your workbench free of any wood chips and grit in the area where your carving is being worked on. If you set your carving over a piece of grit or a small chip of wood as you are working on the carving, it will leave a slight impression in the face of the carving. These marks will show on your carving when the final finish is applied. I realize that I have repeated this warning a few times in the previous steps, but I am trying to avoid a situation where I know that you will be upset to see these marks on your finished work.

I use a draftsman's brush to keep my table top free of anything that would mark my carvings.

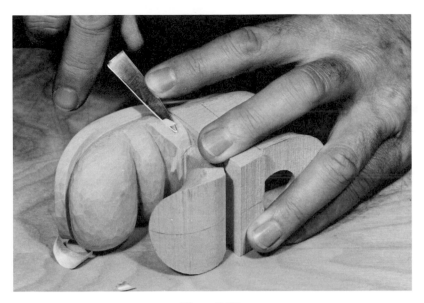

Illus. 9-35

Step 18 in progress.

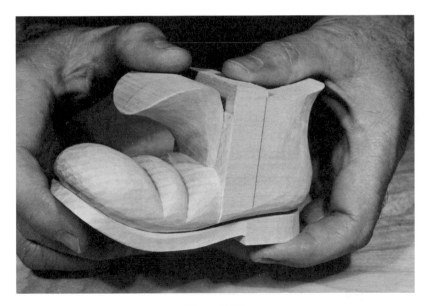

Illus. 9-36

Step 18 completed.

Step 19

      The sides of the boot will be shaped next. To begin, make a vertical cut on the guideline that is parallel to the line that was cut in step 15. Lay the boot on its side as you did in that step. Use the x-acto knife for this cut.

      This cut is very critical because if it is too deep, it will go through the side wall of the boot. The overcut may not show up now but will definitely appear when the interior of the boot is completed. Take these vertical cuts down in stages, as you are shaping the sides of the boot. When shaping the sides, do not overcut into the raised area where the lace holes are located. Side cut to the vertical line only. The back of the boot should blend with the surfaces of the sides.

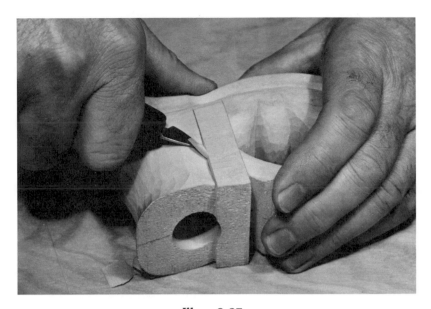

Illus. 9-37

Step 19 in progress.

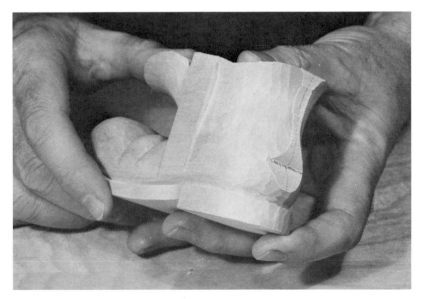

Illus. 9-38

Step 19 completed.

Step 20

The lace hole area, which is raised slightly from the sides of the boot, is completed next. It should be a flowing curved surface that is at its lowest point at the second lace hole location. The highest point of this curved surface is just below the fifth or bottom lace hole. This area is raised a full 1/32 of an inch above the curved surface of the side of the boot. Watch the tip of your carving knife and do not overcut into the sides of the boot.

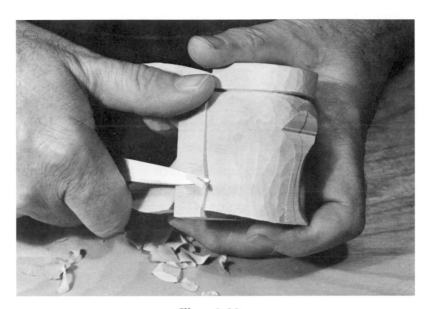

Illus. 9-39

Step 20 in progress.

Illus. 9-40

Step 20 completed.

Step 21

The concave curved portion of the tongue that can be seen from the top view is now shaped. The carver's knife should be as sharp as possible for these cuts. The blade shape, which I have recommended in the chapter for knife making proves to be invaluable for these cuts on the tongue. Do not attempt these cuts with a wide blade because you will not be able to roll the knife as required in this concave area. Start by removing a little wood with each cut, and as you become more familiar with this cut, you can increase the amount of wood that you remove.

Do not "feather" the curved outline of the tongue to a sharp edge. Leave a flat edge of 1/32" around the tongue outline for trimming a little later. See step number 30.

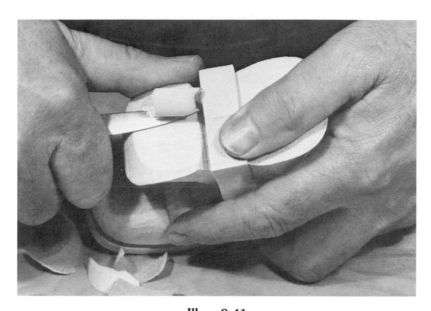

Illus. 9-41

Step 21 in progress.

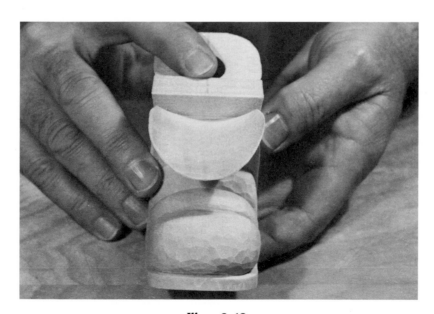

Illus. 9-42

Step 21 completed.

Step 22

      I use a 12 m.m. skew cut chisel to remove the wood between the ⅞″ diameter drilled hole and the concave surface of the tongue. Use the chisel to cut down each side and to remove the wood from the center area. You may prefer to use a gouge for the center area but these are not the final cuts so the gouge is not necessary. You are simply removing some excess wood at this time. Be careful that you do not split the boot at the sides when removing this wood. You must mentally gauge the material thickness at the various points along the sides of the boot, from this point on.

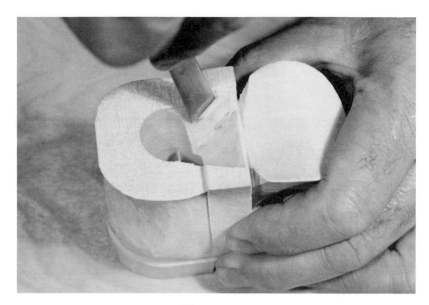

Illus. 9-43

Step 22 in progress.

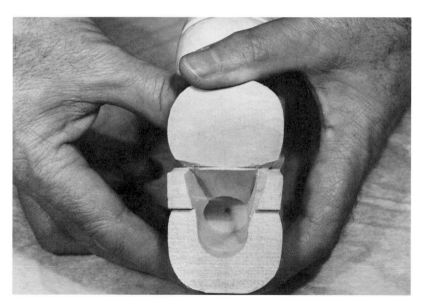

Illus. 9-44

Step 22 completed.

Step 23

The boot is becoming more delicate with each step. Extra care must be exercised when holding the wood carving, and also when performing the remainder of the carving procedures using the knife or chisel.

The 12 m.m. skew chisel is used to reduce the thickness of the areas where the lace holes are located to 3/16". They will be trimmed later, using the carver's knife, to ⅛" thick. The interior face of the tongue is roughed out at the same time that you are cutting down the inside face of the lace hole area. You must control the tip of the chisel at the end of each cut so that you do not leave deep marks at the bottom of the hole.

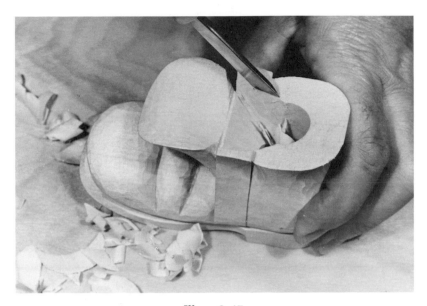

Illus. 9-45

Step 23 in progress.

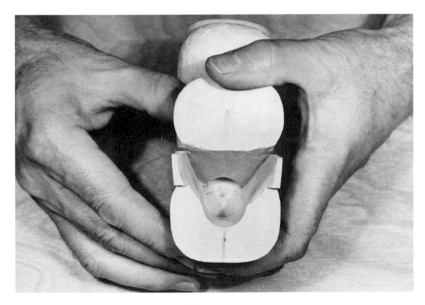

Illus. 9-46

Step 23 completed.

Step 24

       Using the carver's knife, you will start to remove the top portion of the interior of the boot. Follow around the ⅞" drilled hole using the pull cut and the push cut. I find that it is easier to make these cuts if the narrow part of the knife blade, located near the point, is used. You will be using the knife to cut the sides down approximately 1" into the drilled hole. Carve the upper part of the side walls of the boot to the thickness that you will want for your finished boot. I would suggest a thickness of 3/16" for your first boot. Do not feather the top of the boot to a sharp edge. Leave a flat edge of 1/16" which is similar to step 21 for the shaping of the tongue. These edges will be trimmed later. See step 30.

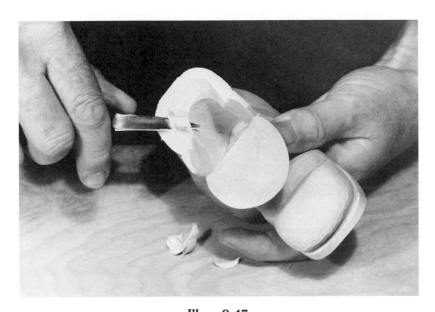

Illus. 9-47

Step 24 in progress.

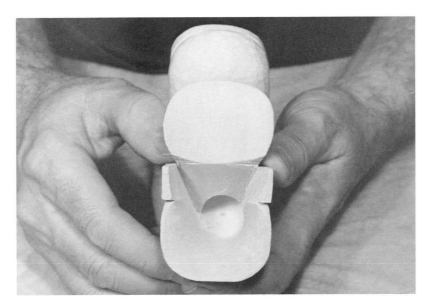

Illus. 9-48

Step 24 completed.

Step 25

The interior walls of the boot are trimmed down at this point. I use a No. 7 gouge which is 14 m.m. wide for this procedure. The chisel must be very sharp because you will be cutting across the grain of the wood. If the basswood that you are using is the softer grade, the chisel must be extra sharp to produce a clean cut. I have found that basswood can vary considerably in hardness. The harder the basswood, the smoother the cut which can be achieved with sharp chisels and knives.

Make these vertical chisel cuts while holding the boot firmly on the top of the workbench with the other hand. Take these vertical cuts down to the bottom of the drilled hole. Make the wall thickness approximately 3/16" thick for your first carving.

Next, remove the ridge that forms between the vertical chisel cuts and the knife cuts from step 24. The carver's knife works very well here.

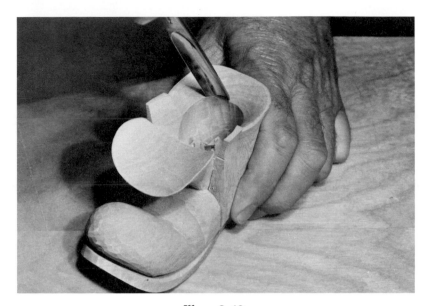

Illus. 9-49

Step 25 in progress.

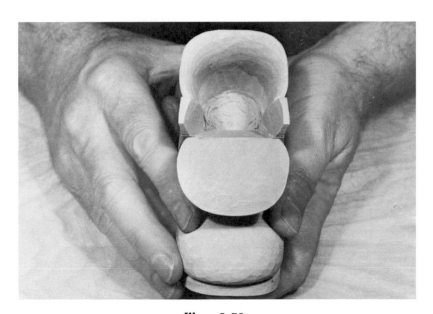

Illus. 9-50

Step 25 completed.

Step 26

There is a straight cut to be made at the point where the tongue ends inside the boot. The cut is vertical and it is taken down to the bottom of the drilled hole.

At the point where the tongue meets the boot, the thickness of the tongue should be 7/16".

The cut in this step can be made with a 12 m.m. wide straight chisel. The problem with trying to make a cut such as this with a straight chisel, is that the corners of the chisel tend to dig into the face of the cut. There is a mark that is left on the face of the wood after each cut, and it is very difficult to prevent this from happening.

The use of a 2 or 3 sweep gouge will prevent these marks from appearing on this vertical cut because each chisel cut with the gouge, overlaps the previous cut. This same principle applies to relief carving, where the straight chisel would not be selected to carve the background for this type of carving. A shallow or deep gouge would be used instead, depending on the texture required for your carving.

Illus. 9-51

Step 26 in progress.

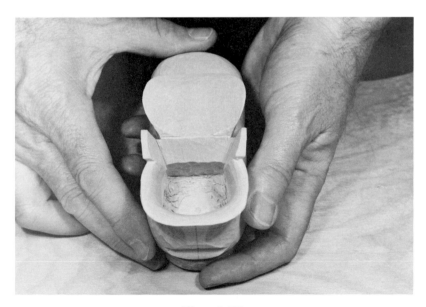

Illus. 9-52

Step 26 completed.

Step 27

The concave surface of the tongue is completed next. Both the carver's knife and a No. 5 gouge which is 16 m.m. wide, are used to carve this area of the boot.

The gouge is only used to shape the lower portion of the tongue. In step 21, you had shaped the front part of the concave surface of the tongue. It is at this point, where the tongue was partially completed, that you start to use the gouge.

The gouge should be held at an angle of 45 degrees as you shape this lower part of the tongue. The height of the curved portion between the lace hole area and the tongue that was established in step 18, will determine how far the concave surface of the tongue will be cut into the boot. This concave surface must become flat as it reaches the straight line that was formed in the previous step.

There is a ridge that still remains on the concave surface of the tongue between the knife cuts formed in step 21 and the cuts from the gouge which have just been completed.

Use a sharp carver's knife to finish this area. These concave knife cuts must be made with a smooth rolling action to provide the best cuts possible for this most important area of the boot carving.

Do not apply too much pressure on the tongue because it could break off at the base. Do not grip the tongue or put any pressure on this area while attempting to hold the carving for the remaining steps of the carving.

Illus. 9-53

Step 27 in progress.

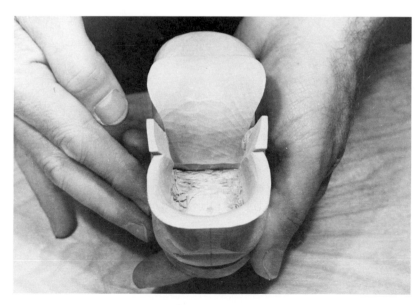

Illus. 9-54

Step 27 completed.

Step 28

The bottom of the boot opening is now carved flat. The center point mark made by the Forstner bit must also be removed at this time. For this procedure, I use a No. 3 spoon gouge 8 m.m. wide, a No. 3 gouge which is 8 m.m. wide and an 8 m.m. straight chisel.

The No. 3 spoon gouge is used to remove the wood from the bottom of the hole. The No. 3 gouge is used to trim the wood along the interior wall where it meets the bottom of the opening. The straight chisel is used to trim at the two corners inside the boot.

When using the spoon gouge, you must cut toward the back of the boot for half of the bottom face, and then toward the tongue for the remaining half. Avoid marking the inside face of the boot with the spoon gouge as you are carving the bottom face.

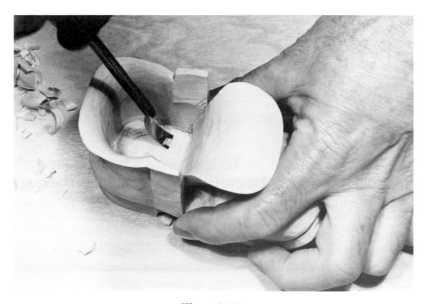

Illus. 9-55

Step 28 in progress.

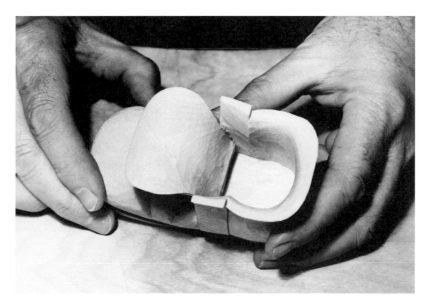

Illus. 9-56

Step 28 completed.

Step 29

There is a small wedge shaped section of wood that still remains on each side of the tongue. It is located between the tongue and the lace hole area of the boot.

I use a long pointed knife blade to remove this wood. After you have removed this wedged shape piece of wood, it will probably be necessary to make a few cuts at the two corners at the base of the tongue. It is difficult to describe the condition that arises when these wedge shaped areas are removed, but it will be obvious to you and just what you must do to correct this situation.

You may find that you can remove this wedge shaped piece of wood with your own choice of tools for example, a 4 m.m. straight chisel etc.

Whatever carving tool you decide to use, be careful, when removing these wedge shaped sections, that you do not leave tool marks on the finished faces at the top of the toe and on the raised area directly behind the toe.

I must admit that I accidentally mark this area every once in awhile with the corner of the knife handle. When I speak of the corner of the knife handle, I am referring to the part of the handle where the blade of the knife meets the handle. These are always small marks and I remove them with a few small knife cuts.

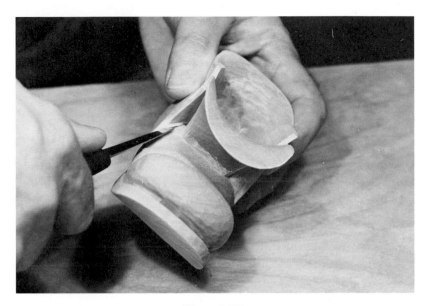

Illus. 9-57

Step 29 in progress.

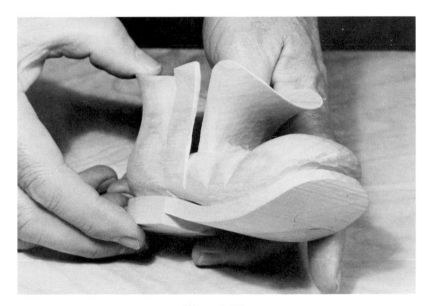

Illus. 9-58

Step 29 completed.

Step 30

     In step 21, a 1/32″ flat edge was left on the curved outline of the tongue which was to be trimmed later. A 1/16″ flat edge was also left on the top edge of the side walls of the boot in step 24. The carver's knife will now be used to finish these edges.

     The edges around the tongue will be done first. Trim the curved front section of the tongue, cutting away just enough wood to remove the flat edge. Now trim the edges of the tongue that go into the boot and to the base of the tongue. If you find that the finished edges appear too wide, you can reduce this width by cutting the curved surface on the underside of the tongue near the edge.

     Trim the front edge and the top edge of the raised lace hole area next. Start with a flat edge and then cut a small bevel or chamfer all around these edges to remove the sharp corners. Note that there are small 45 degree cuts to be made at the corners where the front and top edges meet.

     Proceed to trim the top edge of the side walls of the boot as you did for the tongue.

     The finished edges on the tongue and on the side walls of the boot should be 1/32″ wide when completed.

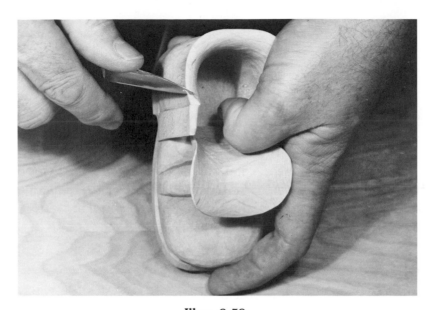

Illus. 9-59

Step 30 in progress.

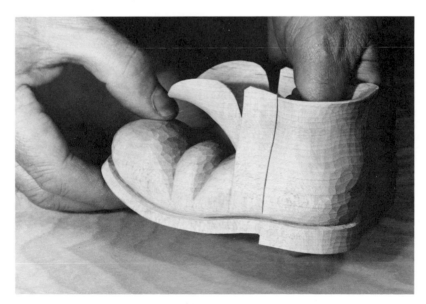

Illus. 9-60

Step 30 completed.

Step 31

There is a raised seam cover at the back of a leather boot which I try to duplicate on the wood carving. This seam cover on the carving is 9/16" wide and it is raised approximately 1/16".

Cut the two vertical lines which are located 9/32" on each side of the center line that you had originally drawn. These two vertical cut lines should be 3/32" deep.

Be careful that you do not cut through the wall of the boot as you are making these vertical cuts.

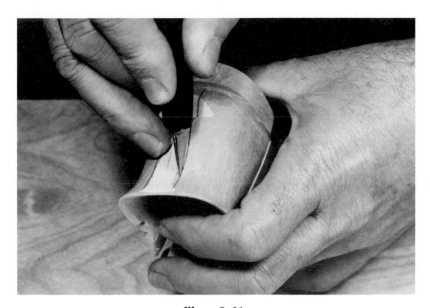

Illus. 9-61

Step 31 in progress.

Step 32

Using the carver's knife, you side cut to these lines to raise this seam area. A short blade knife is much better for this side cutting procedure because you have more control when you use a shorter blade. Do not overcut into this raised area on the back because it will cause chipping along the vertical lines. You will want these vertical lines to look as clean as possible.

The surface of this raised area still has the bandsaw marks on it. Carve this surface just enough to remove these bandsaw marks.

Make the final trim cuts at the top of this raised area.

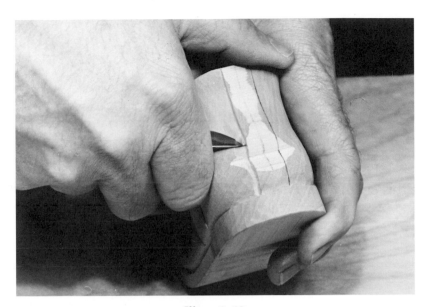

Illus. 9-62

Step 32 in progress.

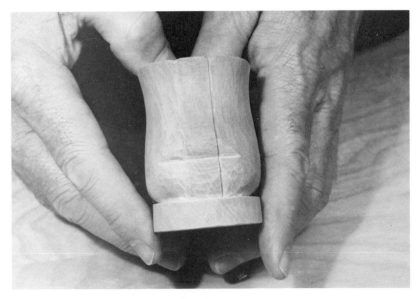

Illus. 9-63

Step 32 completed.

Step 33

There is a curved line which starts at the raised area on the back of the boot and ends up at the sole of the boot. This curved line is shown on the side views of the boots in Illus. 6-1 and 6-2.

Cut a vertical line starting from the raised area at the back of the boot, to a point which is approximately 3/8" short of the sole.

Now starting at the line of the sole, connect this vertical cut to the cut that you have just made.

Now it is just a matter of side cutting on both sides of this vertical cut to form the V shaped groove that you wish to end up with. Round off the high points where the V shaped groove meets the sides of the boot.

Be careful when cutting this curved line that you do not cut through the wall of the boot, especially in the thin areas.

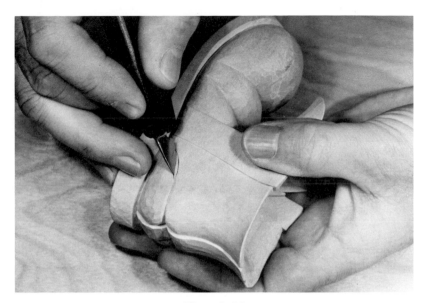

Illus. 9-64

Step 33 in progress.

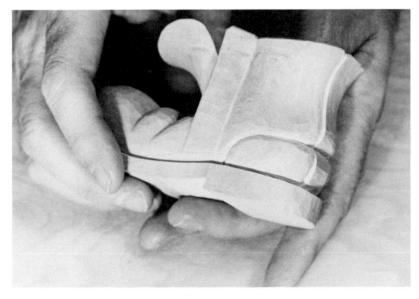

Illus. 9-65

Step 33 completed.

Step 34

The vertical bandsaw cut which is still exposed on the straight edge of the heel, and the entire bottom surface of the sole must be cleaned up with the carver's knife.

The vertical edge on the heel is done first. Next, starting at the high point of the sole, clean the entire bottom surface of the sole toward the toe.

Starting at the same high point on the sole, you now work back to where the sole and the heel meet.

You may wish to carve the flat face of the heel to show cut marks similar to those on the sole. In this way, all of the surfaces of the boot will have cut marks.

The planed surface of the heel that you originally started with, may not be acceptable in the category of "unsanded finish" for some carving show entries.

As your finishing cut, remove the sharp corner that is all around the edge of the heel and the sole.

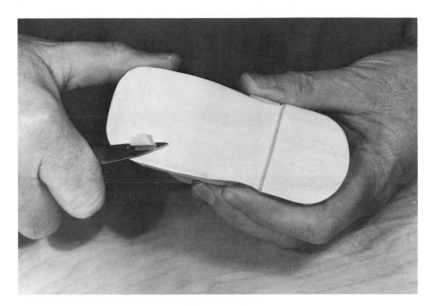

Illus. 9-66

Step 34 in progress.

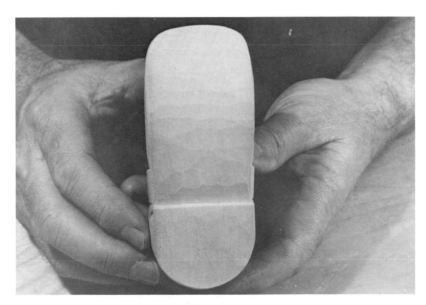

Illus. 9-67

Step 34 completed.

DRILLING THE LACE HOLES

To lay out the centers of the lace holes, you must start by drawing a very light center line that runs parallel with the raised portion of the boot on which the holes are located. I will refer to this line as the vertical center line although it is on an incline. All five holes are spaced evenly on this center line. Start the spacing from the top of the boot. The distance from the top edge to the center of the first hole on the small boot is 3/16″. The distance from the top edge to the center of the first hole on the large boot is ⅜″.

It is important that you locate the center of the fifth or last hole next. To do this, you must hold the pencil point on the vertical center line at the approximate location of this hole. While holding the pencil point on this center, view the boot from the front to see if the hole will clear the curved area between the lace hole and the tongue. Mark this point on both sides of the boot in the same way. Now divide the distance between the center of the first hole and the center of the fifth hole in half. This locates the third hole. To locate the second and the fourth hole you will use the same principle. Divide the distance between the first and third hole in half to locate the second hole. Divide the distance between the third and fifth hole in half to locate the fourth hole.

Never try to locate the holes starting at the first hole and working down to the fifth hole using an arbitrary spacing. You could end up with the fifth hole located too low and it is possible that you may drill into the curved area of the boot just inside of this hole. Use an awl or a steel point that is not too sharp to mark these points (Illus. 10-1).

I suggest a dull steel point because it leaves a large mark on the center of the hole. This helps to keep the drill bit from skipping off the center mark when you start drilling.

I use a 3/32" drill bit for the small boot lace holes and a 5/32" drill bit for the large boot lace holes. Use sharp drill bits to give you the cleanest hole possible.

I prefer to use a high speed drill because it provides a cleaner hole when used with a sharp drill bit. Do not exert very much pressure when drilling. Ease the drill bit through the wood and do not allow the wood to break out on the opposite side (Illus. 10-2).

When drilling the fifth hole, you must stop the drill bit as soon as it makes its way through the wood. At certain angles, when you are drilling this hole, the drill bit could mark the curved area just beyond the hole.

When drilling basswood you will find that the hole will usually require a little cleaning up with fine sandpaper. I cut a sheet of 120 grit sandpaper into 1¼" × 1¼" squares and roll one piece tightly around a round wooden toothpick. Remove the toothpick while holding the sandpaper to this shape. This sandpaper cylinder is inserted into each hole and revolved back and forth between the thumb and forefinger (Illus. 10-3).

Remove any pencil traces of the vertical center line that you had drawn at the start. If not removed, they will show through when the final finish is applied on the boot.

Inspect the carving for any marks or dirt smudges which may have occurred while you were carving. Clean these areas with small knife cuts or, if you prefer, with a light touch of 120 grit sandpaper.

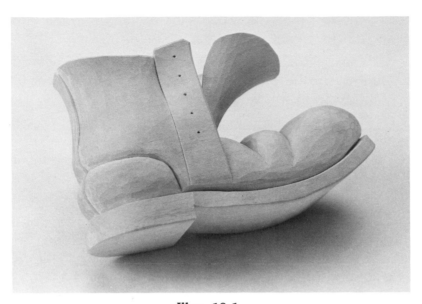

Illus. 10-1

The five lace holes have been laid out on the center line and marked with a steel point.

Illus. 10-2

Drilling the lace holes with a hobby drill.

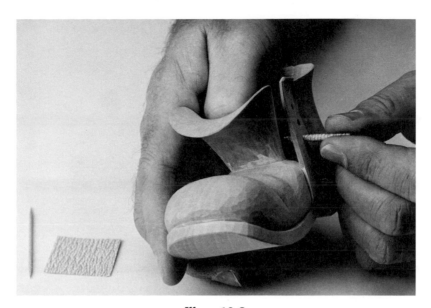

Illus. 10-3

Cleaning out the drilled hole with sandpaper rolled into a cylindrical shape.

FINISHING
THE CARVING

There are many types of finishes which can be used to finish a wood carving. I believe that, during my fifteen years of woodcarving and musical instrument making, I have tried just about every one of them.

For the boot carving, I have received more compliments from both carvers and customers when I have used the simplest finishing method. When I reveal my finishing method to other wood carvers, they invariably say with surprise, "Is that all you do?"

I use a regular interior penetrating stain which is brushed on in one coat. The two colors most preferred by my customers are nutmeg and walnut. The ladies seem to pick the lighter nutmeg color if the choice is available to them at shows or in the gift stores. The advantage of the brushed on stain is that it does not leave any lap marks. It is also a very fast method of staining, in fact the faster that you can brush the carving, the better.

Before you brush the stain on the boot, you must make something to elevate the boot from the table top. This enables you to brush the entire boot in one operation without the heel and part of the sole sticking to the table top. Any scrap piece of ¼″ or ⅜″ thick plywood or particle board will do. The board must be large enough to hammer four ½″ or ⅝″ long finishing nails through it and to have the boot sit on these four nail points (Illus. 11-1). Two nail points should be located under the heel and the other two nail points should be at the lowest surface of the sole.

THIS IS THE SEQUENCE THAT I FOLLOW WHEN BRUSHING MY BOOTS:

1) Brush the interior of the boot. The bottom of the hole is done first and then up the sides on the inside face only.

2) Brush the outer face of the sides and the back of the boot. Start at the lace hole area, proceed around the back, and finish at the opposite lace hole area.

3) Avoiding the tongue completely, I then brush the toe area starting at the point where the tongue meets the boot. Work forward to the toe.

4) Brush the edges of the sole and the heel.

5) Grasp the tongue at its widest point with the thumb on the right side and the forefinger and second finger on the left side. The toe should be pointing toward you.

6) While holding the tongue, turn the boot over and brush the heel and sole. The toe should still be pointing toward you.

7) While the boot is still in this position, brush the underside of the tongue. Brush the stain right up to the fingertips. There will be a little area on each side of the tongue that you cannot brush while you are holding the tongue.

8) Place the boot on the four nails of your brushing board.

9) Brush the areas on the underside of the tongue where your thumb and fingers had been.

10) Complete the brushing by finishing the top surface of the tongue.

Always check that you have not missed any areas. I allow five days for the stain to dry thoroughly while in a dust free area.

You may wish to sign your carving on the heel or on the sole area. This should be done before the finish is applied. I use a fine black marker type pen, which does not run when the finish is brushed on (Illus. 11-2).

Urethane plastic clear coating is used for the final finish. As I have already stated, I have tried every possible finish available to the woodcarver. My customers still prefer the urethane finished boots because the finish is durable and requires no special care.

Illus. 11-1

A piece of particle board or plywood with four nails protruding through it, serves as a brushing and drying stand for the boot.

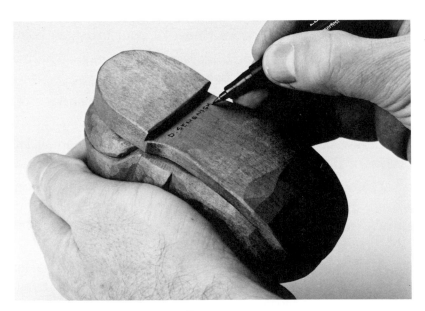

Illus. 11-2

The carver's name can be written on the boot with a fine tip marker type pen after the stain has dried.

I purchase a can of satin finish and a can of flat finish urethane and then mix these two together. I have found that the satin finish, available from most manufacturers, is still too glossy. This mixture of the flat and satin finish has been very popular and has become my standard finish.

The boot carving will require at least two coats of urethane finish. Inspect the finish on the top surface of the tongue after two coats have been applied, to see if a third coat is necessary. This area of the tongue is where the end grain of the wood occurs and it will absorb the urethane finish more readily than some other areas of the boot. If the sheen on the finish does not look uniform, then a third coat will be necessary.

Do not compromise on the brush that you purchase. I use an artist's sable hair brush which is ½″ or ⅝″ wide. These sable hair brushes are very expensive but I find that the finish goes on much smoother and without any trace of brush marks when I use these brushes.

After all of the work that is involved in creating a carving, it would be foolish to use cheap and inferior materials at this final stage of your work.

LACING
THE BOOT

The size of the lace for the small boot is approximately 26″ long × 3/32″ wide and 36″ long × 5/32″ wide for the large boot. I use a flat lace rather than the round lace for my boot carvings because the flat lace hugs the outer face of the boot when the lacing is completed. The round lace tends to stick out from the boot when it is laced through the second hole and hung down the outer face of the boot. This is a small point and it can be overcome by using a very soft round lace. Unfortunately the round lace which is available in most leather craft shops is very stiff.

I purchase scrap pieces of leather, of a suitable color and thickness from leather craft shops and cut my own flat lace. This is far more economical than buying spools of lace ready cut.

You will need a pair of scissors especially made to cut leather (Illus. 12-1). They can be purchased at any leather craft store and are well worth the price. I have cut many laces with my scissors and they are as sharp as the day that I bought them. Use them for cutting your leather lace only and not as a pair of garden pruning shears, and they will last a lifetime.

If you buy a piece of leather with square corners, you must round the corners to approximately a 2″ radius. This will allow you to cut around the entire perimeter of the piece of leather in one continuous operation to produce the lengths of lace that you require. If the corners were left square, sharp kinks would appear on the finished lace.

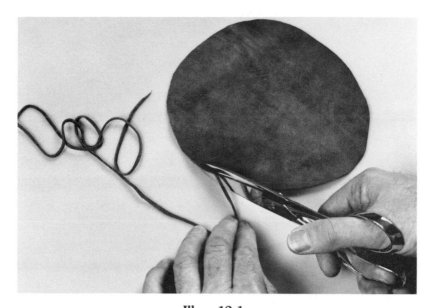

Illus. 12-1

Cutting the leather lace using scissors especially made to cut leather.

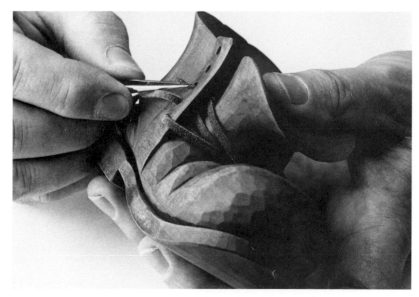

Illus. 12-2

Starting to lace the boot carving.

Illus. 12-3

The boot carving completely laced with the name card tied on the top hole.

If you happen to buy a small piece of leather, let us say 8″ square, then the best approach is to cut this into an 8″ diameter circle. Now you can make a continuous piece of lace by cutting around the perimeter and ending up almost at the center of the piece.

Cut a sharp tip at both ends of the lace that you will be using on your boot. This will allow the end of the lace to be inserted through each hole much easier. I also use a pair of pointed tweezers to pull the stubborn lace ends through the holes as I am lacing up the boot carving.

The lacing is started at the bottom holes and finished at the second holes down from the top (Illus. 12-2). Always lace each hole from the inside of the boot, and then around the face of the tongue and through the next hole up on the opposite side.

When using a flat lace, keep the lace from twisting as you feed it through each hole and across the face of the tongue. I think that this adds to the finished carving, a certain sense of pride that you have in your work.

When you have completed the lacing, the pointed ends along with the excess lengths of lace on both sides of the boot should be cut off. Don't cut the hanging lace ends so that they touch the table top. I have my lace approximately ⅜″ short of the bottom of the boot. In this way, they hang straight down without buckling at the sides.

The top hole of the boot is the ideal location to tie on a card which indicates the name of the carver and whatever other information that you may wish to convey to the prospective buyer. The name card does add a professional touch to your carving (Illus. 12-3).

★　★　★　★

Congratulations for completing this carving project. I hope that you are proud of your first effort.

FRACTIONS OF AN INCH
EXPRESSED AS MILLIMETRES

Fractional inch	mm.	Fractional inch	mm.
$1/64$	0.3969	$33/64$	13.0969
$1/32$	0.7938	$17/32$	13.4938
$3/64$	1.1906	$35/64$	13.8906
$1/16$	1.5875	$9/16$	14.2875
$5/64$	1.9844	$37/64$	14.6844
$3/32$	2.3812	$19/32$	15.0812
$7/64$	2.7781	$39/64$	15.4781
$1/8$	3.175	$5/8$	15.875
$9/64$	3.5719	$41/64$	16.2719
$5/32$	3.9688	$21/32$	16.6688
$11/64$	4.3656	$43/64$	17.0656
$3/16$	4.7625	$11/16$	17.4625
$13/64$	5.1594	$45/64$	17.8594
$7/32$	5.5562	$23/32$	18.2562
$15/64$	5.9531	$47/64$	18.6531
$1/4$	6.35	$3/4$	19.05
$17/64$	6.7469	$49/64$	19.4469
$9/32$	7.1438	$25/32$	19.8438
$19/64$	7.5406	$51/64$	20.2406
$5/16$	7.9375	$13/16$	20.6375
$21/64$	8.3344	$53/64$	21.0344
$11/32$	8.7312	$27/32$	21.4312
$23/64$	9.1281	$55/64$	21.8281
$3/8$	9.525	$7/8$	22.225
$25/64$	9.9219	$57/64$	22.6219
$13/32$	10.3188	$29/32$	23.0188
$27/64$	10.7156	$59/64$	23.4156
$7/16$	11.1125	$15/16$	23.8125
$29/64$	11.5094	$61/64$	24.2094
$15/32$	11.9062	$31/32$	24.6062
$31/64$	12.3031	$63/64$	25.0031
$1/2$	12.7	1	25.4